American English File

Third Edition

4

WORKBOOK

Christina Latham-Koenig
Clive Oxenden

Paul Seligson and Clive Oxenden
are the original co-authors of
English File 1 and *English File* 2

OXFORD
UNIVERSITY PRESS

Contents

How to use your Workbook and Online Practice

American English File
Third Edition

Student Book

Use your Student Book in class with your teacher.

IN CLASS

ACTIVITIES AUDIO VIDEO RESOURCES

AT HOME

Sold separately

ONLINE

Go to americanenglishfileonline.com and use your **Digital Materials Access Code** to log Into the Online Practice.

Workbook

Practice *Grammar*, *Vocabulary*, and *Pronunciation* for every lesson.

Online Practice

← Look again at the Grammar, Vocabulary, and Pronunciation from the Student Book before you do the Workbook exercises.

→ Listen to the audio for the Pronunciation exercises.

→ Use the Sound Bank video to practice English sounds.

Practice the *Colloquial English*.

← Watch the Colloquial English video before you do the exercises.

→ Use the interactive video for more Colloquial English practice.

Do the ***Can you remember...?*** exercises to check that you remember the Grammar, Vocabulary, and Pronunciation every two Files.

→ Look again at the Grammar, Vocabulary, and Pronunciation if you have any problems.

Practice Reading, Listening, Speaking, and Writing.

1A Questions and answers

Judge a man by his questions rather than by his answers.
Voltaire, 18th-century French author, humanist, rationalist, and satirist

G question formation   **V** figuring out meaning from context   **P** intonation: showing interest

1 GRAMMAR question formation

a Right (✓) or wrong (✗)? Correct the mistakes in the highlighted phrases.

1 A You have ever been to Thailand?
   ✗ *Have you ever been*
   B Yes, a couple of times.

2 A Why didn't you tell me the truth?
   ✓ _____
   B Because I thought you'd be angry.

3 A Where you usually go on vacation?
   _____
   B We usually go to Mexico.

4 A Haven't you done the homework?
   _____
   B No, I haven't. I'm sorry.

5 A What did happen at the meeting yesterday?
   _____
   B We discussed the sales figures. It was kind of boring.

6 A Who's Jack going out with?
   _____
   B He's going out with his best friend's sister.

7 A Who fixed your car for you?
   _____
   B My brother.

8 A Whose jacket you did borrow for the wedding?
   _____
   B My dad's. It was a little big for me.

9 A It's late. We should go now?
   _____
   B Yes, we have to get up early tomorrow morning.

10 A For who are you waiting?
   _____
   B I'm waiting for my brother.

b Complete the indirect questions and sentences.

1 "Would Michael like this wallet?"
   Do you think *Michael would like this wallet* _____ ?
2 "Where is the elevator?"
   Could you tell me _____ ?
3 "Where did we park the car?"
   I can't remember _____ .
4 "Are there any tickets left for the concert tonight?"
   Do you know _____ ?
5 "What time does the game start?"
   Can you tell me _____ ?
6 "When's Anna's birthday?"
   Do you remember _____ ?
7 "What does Jamie do for a living?"
   Do you have any idea _____ ?
8 "Where does Natalie live?"
   I wonder _____ .
9 "What's Ava's boyfriend's name?"
   I'm not sure _____ .
10 "How much did you pay for your new car?"
   Would you mind telling me _____ ?

c Write the questions.

1 how long / you / spend / in Brazil last summer
How long did you spend in Brazil last summer ?

2 who / cook / in your family
_____ ?

3 when / your brother / pass / his driver's test
_____
_____ ?

4 you know / who / go / to the party tonight
_____
_____ ?

5 who / the manager / talk to / now
_____
_____ ?

6 who / drink / the milk / I / leave / in the refrigerator
_____
_____ ?

7 why / you / not come / to school yesterday
_____
_____ ?

8 you remember / what time / the meeting / be
_____
_____ ?

d Write questions to ask at a job interview. Use a different phrase to begin each question.

1 salary
_____ ?

2 vacation
_____ ?

3 working hours
_____ ?

4 overtime
_____ ?

5 travel
_____ ?

6 uniform
_____ ?

7 parking space
_____ ?

8 lunch
_____ ?

2 PRONUNCIATION intonation: showing interest

a 🔊 1.1 Listen to the questions. Check (✓) if the speaker sounds interested.

1 Which university did you go to? ✓
2 What don't you like about your job? ☐
3 How's your family? ☐
4 Would you like to work abroad? ☐
5 How many languages do you speak? ☐
6 Why did you leave your last job? ☐

b 🔊 1.2 Listen and repeat the questions with interested intonation.

c Complete the table with the expressions and questions in the list.

~~How interesting!~~   I'm sorry.   Me too!   Oh, really?
What a shame!   Why (not)?   Why do you say that?
Why's that?   Wow!

Expressions showing interest
How interesting!
Expressions showing sympathy
Follow-up questions

d 🔊 1.3 Listen and check. Then listen again and repeat the expressions.

e 🔊 1.4 Now listen to the questions from **a** in conversations. Complete the phrases or questions that people use to react to the answers.

1 *Me too!* When were you there?
2 _____ How long have you been there?
3 _____ I hope it's nothing serious.
4 _____ What's keeping you here?
5 _____ That's a lot of languages.
6 _____ I'm sorry to hear that.

f 🔊 1.5 Listen and repeat the responses. Copy the intonation.

🔄 **Go online** for more practice

3 READING & VOCABULARY figuring out meaning from context

a Complete the sentences with the words and phrases in the list.

> foolproof geek good-natured rivalry
> gut feeling job-seekers light-hearted response
> the point of work–life balance

1 Josh is a computer _geek_____, so he's been applying for jobs in IT.
2 If someone tries to annoy me, I prefer to give a _____ rather than get angry.
3 My colleague and I enjoy a _____ over who meets our monthly targets first.
4 Great news for _____: more than 50% of US companies intend to hire new staff this year.
5 I have a _____ that this interview will go very badly.
6 I don't see _____ some interview questions – they seem ridiculous.
7 It can be difficult to get the right _____, especially if you have a position of responsibility in a company.
8 This article gives five _____ tips on how to be successful at a job interview.

b Read the article quickly. Match the **bold** words in the highlighted phrases to definitions 1–8.

1 (*adj.*) extremely useful
invaluable
2 (*adj.*) done very carefully, with attention to detail
_____
3 (*adj.*) possible
_____
4 (*phrasal verb*) be noticeable because of being different
_____
5 (*verb*) sit in a lazy way, with your shoulders bent forwards
_____
6 (*phrase*) avoid
_____
7 (*adj.*) real; true
_____
8 (*verb*) keep touching something because you are nervous
_____

Important interview tips

Your résumé got you in the door; now it's time to convince the interviewer you're the best person for the job.

Research the company
Do your homework so you don't give the impression you're looking for any old job. Search the Internet and read not only the company's website, but also any news stories that come up. Make a list of points you could discuss at the interview and questions you could ask. You want your **potential** future **employer** to believe that you have a **genuine** interest in working for the organization.

Look the part
The company's dress code should give you an idea of what to wear at the interview, but in most cases, you will be expected to look professional. However, it is not only your clothes you must watch. Think about your body language: do you usually **slouch** or sit up straight in a chair, or do you sometimes **fiddle** with a pen? Practice before the day so that you have time to replace any bad habits with positive body language.

Mind your manners
When you get to the interview venue, make sure you greet everyone you meet, including the people in the elevator. Offer the interviewer a warm greeting and say "please" and "thank you" when appropriate. Not only do you want to show that you would be an **invaluable** team member, but you also want the interviewer to choose you over another candidate who may be equally qualified for the job.

Give real examples
You won't be the first candidate the interviewer has met, so you need to **stand out** from the competition. When you are asked about your abilities and experience, **steer clear** of typical answers such as "I have great communication skills" or "I'm a people person." Instead give real examples of situations where you have demonstrated these qualities and brought about a positive result.

Ask the right questions
Towards the end of the interview, you will be invited to ask your own questions about the job. You'll have that list you made beforehand, but the points on it may already have been covered. Even if the interviewer has been very **thorough**, you must ask a few questions. This is where your initial research about the company will come in handy.

Go online for more practice

G auxiliary verbs, *the...*, *the... + comparatives* | **V** compound adjectives, modifiers | **P** intonation and sentence rhythm

1 GRAMMAR auxiliary verbs

a Cross out the unnecessary words.

1 My mom can drive, but my dad can't ~~drive~~.
2 I loved that book, but my wife didn't love that book.
3 You weren't listening to the instructions, but I was listening to the instructions.
4 Some people believe in ghosts, but others don't believe in ghosts.
5 Gina's going to the party, but Robbie isn't going to the party.
6 I always lock the front door, but my partner doesn't always lock the front door.
7 I've never been to a fortune-teller, but my sister has visited a fortune-teller.
8 My friends had already heard the story, but I hadn't already heard the story.

b Complete the conversations with a tag question or an auxiliary.

1 **A** I texted you last night, but you didn't reply.
 B I *did* reply. I texted you right away.

2 **A** I don't feel like cooking tonight.
 B Neither _____ I. Let's go out for dinner. I'd love some Mexican food.
 A So _____ I. Come on. Let's go.

3 **A** I've seen this movie before.
 B Well, I _____.
 A Do you mind if I change channels?
 B Yes, I _____ mind! I want to see the end.

4 **A** You're going to Sam's party, _____ you?
 B No, I'm not.
 A Why not? You haven't argued with him again, _____ you?
 B Yes. We aren't going out together anymore.

5 **A** I'll be back a little bit late tonight.
 B You _____ ? Where are you going?
 A To a concert with some friends.
 B Oh, OK. You'll be back before 12, _____ you?
 A Of course.

6 **A** You couldn't lend me some money, _____ you?
 B No, sorry. Why?
 A I spent my entire salary already this month.
 B So _____ I!

7 **A** I didn't go out last night.
 B Neither _____ I. I was too tired.
 A So _____ I!

8 **A** You aren't from around here, _____ you?
 B No, I'm from Australia.
 A I don't suppose you like this cold weather.
 B Actually, I _____ like it. I prefer cool weather to hot weather.

c Respond to the statements with *So do I, Neither do I, I do, I don't,* etc., and say why.

1 I didn't go out yesterday.
 _____

2 I love the ocean.
 _____

3 I've never been to Canada.
 _____

4 I'd like to go on a safari.
 _____

5 I wasn't interested in history in school.
 _____

6 I'm good at languages.
 _____

7 I can swim well.
 _____

8 I don't exercise at all.
 _____

2 PRONUNCIATION intonation and sentence rhythm

a 🔊 1.6 Listen and complete the conversations.

1 A You *don't* _____ like the soup, *do* _____ you?
  B I *do* _____ like it. It's just that it's very hot.

2 A We _____ invited to their wedding.
  B You _____ ? Neither _____ we.

3 A I _____ enjoy that movie.
  B You _____ ? I _____ .

4 A I _____ always very well behaved as a child.
  B You _____ ? I _____ .

5 A You _____ forget to call me, _____ you?
  B Of course I _____ .

6 A I _____ play tennis well.
  B You _____ ? I _____ .

b 🔊 1.6 Listen again and repeat the conversations. Copy the rhythm and intonation.

3 GRAMMAR IN CONTEXT *the..., the... + comparatives*

Complete the sentences with the comparative form of the adjectives in the list.

big   cold   difficult   ~~early~~   far   ~~good~~   high
interesting   late   likely   long   qualified

1 The *earlier* _____ we set off, the *better* _____ chance we'll have of avoiding the rush hour traffic.
2 The _____ the class, the _____ the students are to learn something.
3 The _____ you go to bed, the _____ it is to get up in the morning.
4 The _____ north you travel in Canada, the _____ it gets.
5 The _____ the person is for the job, the _____ the salary.
6 The _____ your house, the _____ it takes you to clean it.

4 VOCABULARY compound adjectives, modifiers

a Match the definitions to the compound adjectives in the list.

absentminded   ~~bad-tempered~~   big-headed
easygoing   good-tempered   laid-back   narrow-minded
open-minded   self-centered   strong-willed   tight-fisted
two-faced   well-balanced   well-behaved

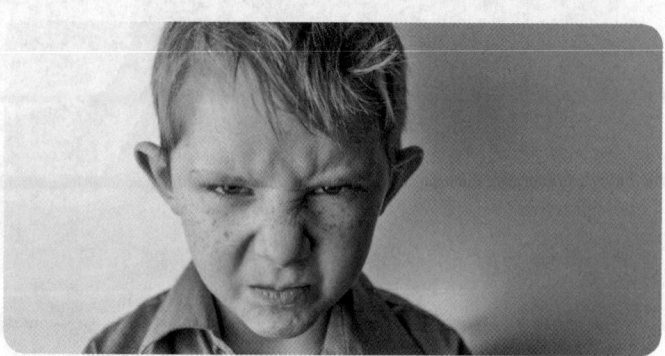

1 easily made angry or annoyed
  bad-tempered _____
2 ready to consider new ideas and opinions
  _____
3 not willing to spend money
  _____
4 often forgetting or not noticing things
  _____
5 determined to do what you want to do, even if other people advise you not to
  _____
6 relaxed; not easily worried by things
  _____
7 sensible and emotionally in control
  _____
8 having a very high opinion of how important and smart you are
  _____
9 not willing to listen to ideas different from your own
  _____
10 dishonest about your feelings; telling people what you think will please them
  _____
11 cheerful and not easily made angry
  _____
12 thinking only about yourself and not about other people
  _____
13 calm; not easily upset by what other people do
  _____
14 behaving in a way that people think is polite and correct
  _____

🔘 **Go online** for more practice

b Complete the sentences with the compound adjectives in **a**.

1 My parents are very *easygoing*_____. They accept most things I do, without getting upset.
2 Tom's wife is very _____. She doesn't seem to let anything worry her.
3 Oliver's new girlfriend isn't as crazy as he is. She seems very _____.
4 My partner is really _____. He won't listen to other people's ideas.
5 Grace never thinks of anyone else because she's so _____.
6 My sister-in-law is very _____. She's nice to me, and then speaks badly of me to other people.
7 Since he went to work abroad for a while, Leo has become more _____ about other cultures.
8 She's very _____, and if she's decided to become a vegetarian, nothing will stop her.
9 When we go out, my friend Jack never offers to pay for gas. I wish he wasn't so _____.
10 The new manager seems very _____. He spent most of the meeting telling us how successful he was.
11 My grandmother never remembers where she's put her keys. She's very _____.
12 I've never seen your children being bad. They're really _____.
13 Our English teacher never seems to get angry. She's extremely _____.
14 It's best not to talk to my brother when he first gets up. He's usually very _____.

c (Circle) the correct answer. Check (✓) if both answers are possible.

1 Tony's new girlfriend is good for him – she seems *rather /* (really) well-balanced. ▢
2 I don't trust my neighbor – she's *extremely / incredibly* two-faced. ✔
3 Some people complain about my kids, but I think they're *pretty / a little* well-behaved. ▢
4 My cousin Olivia is *very / really* tight-fisted – she doesn't want to give any money towards our grandfather's 80th birthday present. ▢
5 I'm not that sure about my new colleague. I find him *really / rather* big-headed. ▢
6 I get along well with my boss. He's *very / rather* easygoing. ▢
7 If I have a problem, I usually talk to my aunt. She's *a kind of / incredibly* open-minded. ▢
8 I don't spend much time with my roommate – she's *a kind of / pretty* self-centered. ▢

d Choose eight of the compound adjectives in **a** and write sentences about yourself. Use a suitable modifier from the list. Explain your answers.

| a little   extremely   incredibly   kind of   pretty |
| rather   really   very |

1 _____
  _____
2 _____
  _____
3 _____
  _____
4 _____
  _____
5 _____
  _____
6 _____
  _____
7 _____
  _____
8 _____
  _____

5 VOCABULARY FROM READING

Complete the missing letters in the words.

1 Detectives are searching for clues to help them s _o_ l _v_ _e_ last night's murder.
2 She told reporters the ex _ _ _ _ r _ _ n _ _ _ story of how she survived the plane crash.
3 It takes six days to reach the r _ m _ _ _ island of Tristan da Cunha by boat.
4 The search party found no tr _ _ _ of the missing climbers.
5 The strange geology of the planet Mars continues to b _ f _ _ _ scientists.

1 Colloquial English Getting a job

1 LOOKING AT LANGUAGE

Complete the sentences with the right form of *make* or *do*.

1 Remember to *make*_____ eye contact when you meet your new manager.

2 Let's _____ a Google search on each of the top five candidates who applied for the job.

3 I _____ a huge mistake on my résumé when I included every job I've had in the past ten years.

4 Did you _____ sure your cell phone was turned off during your job interview?

5 Most employers don't care about what you _____ 20 or 30 years ago.

6 I'm _____ a three-column table in the document so the information is easy to read.

2 VOCABULARY FROM THE INTERVIEW

Match the **bold** word or phrase with the correct definition.

1 ...as an employer, I'm thinking this has no **relevancy** to me
   a agreements
   b connection

2 Dress **appropriately** for an interview.
   a in a suitable way
   b in a stylish, formal suit

3 You can often **stake out** the front door, ...
   a watch secretly
   b watch illegally

4 You don't want to have any **interruptions**.
   a times when an activity is stopped
   b times when an activity begins

5 I can deliver enough **value** for this position...
   a how expensive something is
   b how much something is worth compared with its price

3 THE CONVERSATION

Complete the sentences with one word, using repetition or an adverb to add emphasis.

1 It's a terrible, *terrible*_____ idea to go to an interview when you're feeling hungry.

2 I've _____ told you this before more than once.

3 I felt really, _____ silly when I realized I'd locked my keys in the house.

4 You _____ told me you would be here by 11:00.

5 Can you make me a cup of tea? I've had a _____ bad day.

6 It's a wonderful _____ movie. You really should go and see it.

4 VOCABULARY FROM THE CONVERSATION

Complete the sentences with a word from the list.

caught   potentially   ~~slightly~~   white   willing

1 I sometimes *slightly* exaggerate when I talk about my experience.

2 You might find yourself in a _____ difficult situation.

3 Nobody will worry if you tell a couple of _____ lies.

4 You could get _____ out if they ask you questions about something on your résumé.

5 You need to show that you are _____ to learn.

Can you remember...? 1

GRAMMAR & VOCABULARY

a Complete the second sentence so that it means the same as the first sentence. Use the word in parentheses. Contractions are one word.

1 My husband and I both love animals. (so)
   I love animals and _so_____ _does_____
   _my_____ _husband_____.

2 I'm sure I sent you a message last night. (did)
   I _did_____ _send_____ _you_____
   _a_____ _message_____ last night.

3 Whose is this phone? (belong)
   Who _____ _____ _____
   _____ to?

4 What was wrong with the hotel you stayed in? (like)
   Why _____ _____ _____ the
   hotel you stayed in?

5 Where did you get that book from? (gave)
   _____ _____ _____ that book?

6 How much is gas in your country? (costs)
   Do you know _____ _____
   _____ _____ in your country?

7 Do you have any vacancies right now? (whether)
   Can you _____ _____ _____
   _____ _____ any vacancies right now?

8 I'm just checking that you'll pick me up from work tonight. (you)
   You will pick me up from work tonight, _____
   _____?

9 My friends and I can't afford to go on vacation this year. (neither)
   I can't afford to go on vacation this year and
   _____ _____ _____
   _____.

10 I'm sure Tom knows about the meeting – he mentioned it yesterday. (does)
   Tom _____ _____ _____
   _____ _____ – he mentioned it
   yesterday.

b Read the text. Circle a, b, or c.

The Bermuda Triangle

During the 1960s and 70s, many stories were told of ships and aircraft disappearing mysteriously in a region of the Atlantic Ocean known as the Bermuda Triangle. People asked, "[1]____ is causing these boats and planes to disappear?", and several [2]____ reasons were given to explain the mystery. Some writers wondered [3]____ aliens had established an underwater base and were hijacking aircraft to study their crew. Others said that enormous waves might be hitting vessels, causing them to sink without a [4]____. However, nobody asked the question of whether there really [5]____ any mystery to explain.

Journalist Larry Kusche was the first person to do this. He asked questions about the mysterious disappearances that previous writers [6]____. These writers had simply collected stories that had already been written and repeated them in their own way. Kusche found many mistakes in their stories: in some cases, there was no record of the ships and planes that were said to have been lost, and in others, they had disappeared during [7]____ bad storms. Kusche pointed out that it was logical that more accidents would occur in the busy Bermuda Triangle than in more [8]____ areas such as the South Pacific because the more ships there are in an area, the [9]____ it is for one of them to sink.

In the end, Kusche concluded that the explanation for the Bermuda Triangle [10]____ was neither aliens nor massive waves, but the lack of research done by writers in search of a sensational story.

1 **a** How   **b** What   **c** Which
2 **a** foreign   **b** extraordinary **c** absentminded
3 **a** how   **b** whether   **c** where
4 **a** mark   **b** sign   **c** trace
5 **a** is   **b** has   **c** was
6 **a** didn't   **b** hadn't   **c** weren't
7 **a** rather   **b** pretty   **c** extremely
8 **a** crowded   **b** far   **c** remote
9 **a** likely   **b** more likely   **c** most likely
10 **a** puzzle   **b** quiz   **c** story

✓ **Go online** to check your progress

G present perfect simple and continuous   **V** illnesses and injuries   **P** /ʃ/, /dʒ/, /tʃ/, and /k/

1 VOCABULARY illnesses and injuries

a Complete the minor illnesses and injuries.

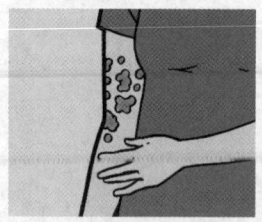

1 She has a r <u>a s h</u>.

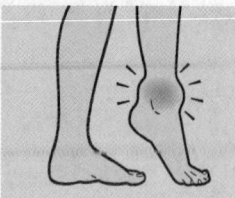

2 Her ankle is s _ _ l _ _ n.

3 She's v _ _ _ t _ _ _ _.

4 Her finger is bl _ _ d _ _ _ _.

5 She has s _ _ b _ _ _ _.

6 She's sn _ _ z _ _ _ _.

7 She has a c _ _ g _.

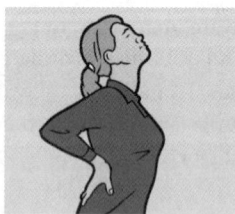

8 Her back h _ _ t _.

9 She has a h _ _ d _ _ c _.

10 She has a t _ _ p _ r _ t _ _ _.

b Complete the sentences.

1 Alex has d*iarrhea*____. He's been to the bathroom six times this morning.
2 I think I have the fl_____. I have a temperature and I ache all over.
3 That knife is very sharp. Please don't c_____ y_____.
4 Matt f_____ in the art gallery. It was so hot that he lost consciousness.
5 These shoes aren't very comfortable. I think I have a bl_____.
6 I have a s_____ thr_____. It hurts when I talk.
7 Rachel f_____ s_____. She thinks she's going to vomit.
8 You're coughing and sneezing a lot. Do you have a c_____?
9 I feel d_____. Everything is spinning around.

c Complete the conversations with a word from the list.

~~allergic reaction~~   blood pressure   burned   choking
food poisoning   sprained   unconscious

1 **P** There's a rash all over my body.
  D You might have had an *allergic reaction*____ to something.

2 **P** Where am I?
  D In the hospital. You had an accident and you've been _____ for an hour.

3 **P** I fell and hurt my wrist playing tennis – now it's very swollen.
  D I think you've _____ it.

4 **P** I sometimes feel a little dizzy when I first get up.
  D It sounds like you have low _____.

5 **P** I've been sick and I have diarrhea.
  D You might have _____. Didn't you say you thought the shrimp you had for lunch weren't fully cooked?

6 **P** What should I do if one of my children starts _____?
  D Tell them not to panic and to keep coughing – they need to move the food.

7 **P** I dropped a pan of boiling water on my hand.
  D Yes, you've _____ yourself very badly.

d Match conditions 1–6 to treatments a–f.

1 an allergic reaction   <u> e </u>
2 a headache   <u>   </u>
3 an infection   <u>   </u>
4 a major cut   <u>   </u>
5 a minor cut   <u>   </u>
6 a sprained ankle   <u>   </u>

a get stitches
b put antibiotic ointment and a Band-Aid™ on it
c put ice on it and bandage it
d take antibiotics
e take antihistamine tablets or cream
f take painkillers

e Complete the sentences with a word from the list.

~~down~~   out   over   around   up

1 You should go and lie <u>*down*</u> if you aren't feeling well.
2 If you stand for too long in this heat, you might pass _____.
3 You shouldn't go out until you get _____ the flu completely.
4 If you think you're going to throw _____, tell me and I'll stop the car.
5 I must have fainted. When I came _____ I was lying on the floor.

f Complete the medical advice with the words in the list.

bandage   damp cloth   ~~pinch~~   press   rub
running water   tip

1 You can stop a nosebleed if you <u>*pinch*</u> the soft part of your nose and _____ your head forward.
2 If you put cool _____ on a burn, it will stop blisters from forming.
3 You shouldn't put a hot _____ on a sprained ankle because the heat will make the ankle more swollen.
4 Don't _____ the arms and legs of someone with hypothermia because you will make them lose more heat.
5 You should only stand behind someone who's choking and _____ their stomach inwards if they can't talk, cough, or breathe.
6 If you put antibiotic ointment and a _____ on a bad cut, you will stop the wound from getting infected.

g Write a short paragraph about your last illness / injury. Include…

- when you were ill / injured and what the illness / injury was.
- what the symptoms were.
- what the treatment was.
- how long it took you to get over it.

2 VOCABULARY FROM READING

Complete the sentences with a phrase from the list.

heart rate   life-threatening illness   ~~miracle cures~~
open-heart surgery   scare stories   under the weather
worst-case scenario

1 Most stories about <u>*miracle cures*</u> are fake news.
2 Ethan is concerned because his _____ gets very high when he exercises.
3 Most people want to know about the _____ when they are diagnosed with an illness, but it's unlikely things will get that bad.
4 It isn't easy for doctors to tell patients that they are suffering from a _____.
5 I've been feeling _____ recently, so I've made an appointment with my doctor.
6 My uncle is very sick in the hospital, and he's going to have _____ tomorrow.
7 Newspapers are full of _____ about what will happen if we eat certain foods.

3 PRONUNCIATION /ʃ/, /dʒ/, /tʃ/, and /k/

a ⟨Circle⟩ the word with a different sound.

1	ʃ shower	1 ⟨chest⟩ infection pressure rash
2	k keys	2 ache cholesterol sick specialist
3	dʒ jazz	3 allergic emergency finger injury
4	tʃ chess	4 choke stitches stomach temperature
5	ʃ shower	5 couch operation shock unconscious
6	dʒ jazz	6 bandage injection negative surgeon

b ◉ 2.1 Listen and check. Then listen again and repeat the words.

Go online for more practice

4 GRAMMAR present perfect simple and continuous

a Right (✓) or wrong (✗)? Correct the mistakes in the highlighted phrases.

1 You don't need to call the doctor – I've already made an appointment for you.

   ✓

2 This is the first time I've been spraining my ankle – I didn't know it hurt so much!

   ✗ *I've sprained my ankle*

3 Mia isn't going to school today because she's been throwing up all night.

4 I've fallen lots of times playing soccer, but I've never broken a bone.

5 I can't take anything for my headache because we've been running out of painkillers.

6 You've been complaining about your back for weeks – why don't you go to the doctor?

7 How long have you been knowing about your grandfather's illness?

8 Sasha's coughed all day, and now he has a sore throat.

9 My sister has a skin problem – she's been going to a doctor for treatment for over two years.

10 How many times have you been fainting recently?

b Complete the sentences using the words in parentheses. Use the present perfect simple or continuous form of the verb. Put the adverbs in the correct position.

1 Jess is a little nervous – *she's never ridden* a horse before. (she / ride / never)

2 How many cookies _____? (you / eat)

3 My brother's really stressed about work, so _____ very well recently. (he / not sleep)

4 _____ my hand on the oven – it really hurts! (I / burn / just)

5 _____ problems with my shoulder for several months now. (I / have)

6 Ed is one of the nicest people _____. (I / meet / ever)

7 _____ to the gym for long – just a few weeks. (Georgia / not go)

8 _____ a sore throat for more than a week now. (Jamie / have)

9 How long _____ a job? (your girlfriend / look for)

10 I bought that book last month, but _____ it yet. (I / not read)

c Complete the email with the correct form of the verbs in parentheses. Use the present perfect simple or continuous.

✉

Hi Junko,

Thanks for your email – it was great to hear from you!

Sorry I ¹*haven't replied* (not reply) until now, but I ² _____ (not feel) very well recently. I ³ _____ (have) the flu, and I'm only just getting over it now. I ⁴ _____ (not go) to work for a week; I ⁵ _____ (lie) on the sofa at home all day. My mom ⁶ _____ (take care of) me all week, and I'm almost better now. I'll probably go back to work the day after tomorrow.

Anyway, I'm so glad you're planning on coming to visit next summer – it will be great to see you! While I've been sick, I ⁷ _____ (think) about what we can do while you're here, and I ⁸ _____ (come up with) a few ideas. I know how much you love music, so for the last few days I ⁹ _____ (try) to get some tickets for a music festival, but I ¹⁰ _____ (not manage) to get any yet. Is there anything else you'd like to do during your visit? I'm really looking forward to seeing you, and I know that we'll have a fantastic time.

Write back soon!

Love,

Aria

---

d Answer Aria's email. Write 140–190 words. Use the present perfect simple and continuous. Include the following:

- thank Aria for her email
- explain why you haven't written until now
- answer Aria's question
- ask Aria a question

🔄 Go online for more practice

If you speak three languages, you are trilingual.
If you speak two, you are bilingual.
If you speak one, you are English.
German joke

G using adjectives as nouns, adjective order **V** clothes and fashion **P** vowel sounds

1 GRAMMAR using adjectives as nouns, adjective order

a Complete the sentences with the noun form of the adjectives in the list.

| blind deaf disabled ~~elderly~~ injured rich |
| unemployed young |

1 Should the family or the state look after *the elderly*?
2 The government is offering courses to help _____ to find jobs.
3 After the accident, _____ were taken to the hospital.
4 The building has easy access for _____.
5 Do you think _____ should pay higher taxes than the poor?
6 In some countries, _____ use special dogs to help them find their way around.
7 _____ always think that they know better than their parents.
8 _____ usually communicate with each other using sign language.

b Complete the sentences with *the* + adjective.

1 *The Vietnamese* usually celebrate Tet in January or February.
2 _____ eat a lot of fish. (Japan)
3 _____ export a lot of electrical products to the rest of the world. (China)
4 _____ have a good standard of living. (Switzerland)
5 _____ are very kind and friendly to visitors. (Portugal)
6 _____ have a reputation for being polite. (England)
7 _____ enjoy spending time outdoors. (Scotland)
8 _____ are extremely fond of bike riding. (France)

c Right (✓) or wrong (✗)? Correct the mistakes in the highlighted phrases.

1 Sarah's wearing a denim short skirt.
   ✗ *a short denim skirt*
2 I'm looking for a sleeveless cotton T-shirt.
   ✓ _____
3 I want to buy some leather white pants.
   _____
4 You can't wear those old scruffy jeans to the wedding.
   _____
5 He gave his mother a patterned silk scarf for her birthday.
   _____
6 He looks very fashionable in his gray new Armani suit.
   _____
7 She was wearing a bright red wool scarf.
   _____
8 My sister bought some purple trendy glasses.
   _____

d Write each pair of sentences as one sentence.

1 My grandparents live in an old brick house. It's big.
   My grandparents live in a big old brick house.

2 I met a Brazilian woman at the party. She was interesting.
   _____

3 My sister has pretty black hair. It's long.
   _____

4 Ava bought an expensive silk top. It's striped.
   _____

5 There's a round wooden table in my friend's kitchen. It's beautiful.
   _____

6 Max gave his girlfriend an unusual ring for her birthday. It's gold.
   _____

7 My boss drives a powerful Italian sports car. It's red.
   _____

8 We've been having some wet weather recently. It's been awful.
   _____

2 VOCABULARY clothes and fashion

a Complete the crossword with the adjectives.

ACROSS →

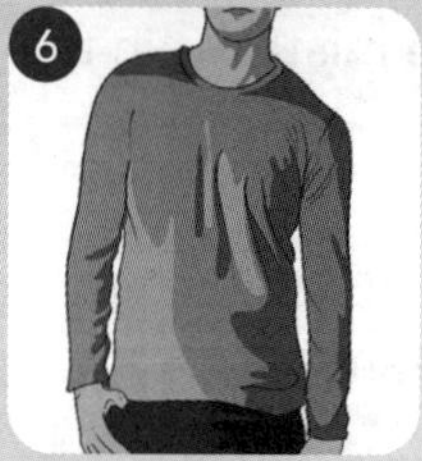

DOWN ↓

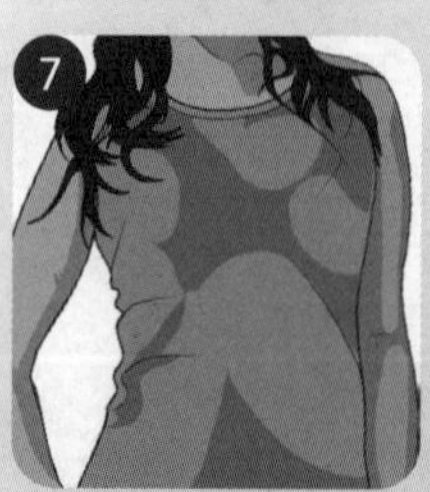

¹P ²L A I N

Go online for more practice

b Order the letters in parentheses to make a material. Then complete the sentences.

1 Jack was wearing a blue *denim* jacket. (NIMED)
2 I prefer to wear light _____ shirts in the summer. (TTNCOO)
3 I gave my mom a blouse with a _____ collar for her birthday. (CEAL)
4 Are you sure those boots are made of _____? (HTRELEA)
5 I never buy _____ clothes because they take so long to iron. (NINLE)
6 They gave me a very expensive _____ tie as a going-away present. (LIKS)
7 Don't wear your _____ jacket out – it's raining. (SEDUE)
8 I really like your new _____ jacket. It looks very soft. (VVTEEL)
9 My aunt often wears a _____ coat, but it isn't real. (URF)
10 I always wear a _____ top in the gym – it's the most comfortable. (CRALY)
11 My grandfather wears an old _____ cardigan around the house in the winter. (OLOW)

c Complete the sentences.

1 You don't have to spend a lot of money to look f*ashionable*.
2 Alice enjoys wearing cl_____ clothes that will never go out of fashion.
3 It isn't a formal dinner, so I'm going to wear something c_____.
4 Zach looked very scr_____ when I saw him: his T-shirt was dirty, and he hadn't combed his hair.
5 You look like my dad in those pants – they're really o_____-f_____.

d Match 1–8 to a–h to make questions.

1 How often do you dress _____*f*_____
2 How many clothes do you have _____
3 Do you get _____
4 When do you get dressed _____
5 Do you always hang _____
6 What color do you think _____
7 Is it important for you that your shoes _____
8 Do you have any clothes that go _____

a suits you best?
b in the morning?
c match your clothes? Why / Why not?
d that don't fit you?
e with everything? What?
f up to go out for a special occasion?
g changed as soon as you get home from work / school? Why / Why not?
h up your clothes before you go to bed?

e Answer the questions in **d**.

1 _____
2 _____
3 _____
4 _____
5 _____
6 _____
7 _____
8 _____

3 PRONUNCIATION vowel sounds

a Circle the word with a different sound.

![boot]	![fish]	![bird]	![bike]	![train]
1	2	3	4	5
boot	fish	bird	bike	train
loose	linen	fur	fit	lace
scruffy	slippers	shirt	Lycra	leather
shoes	silk	shorts	stylish	plain
suit	striped	skirt	tight	suede

b 🔊 2.2 Listen and check. Then listen again and repeat the words.

🔗 **Go online** for more practice   ✓ **Go online** to check your progress

Fasten your seat belts

I don't have a fear of flying;
I have a fear of crashing.
Billy Bob Thornton, American actor

G narrative tenses, past perfect continuous, *so / such...that...* **V** air travel **P** irregular past forms, sentence rhythm

1 VOCABULARY air travel

a Replace the **bold** words with a formal word or phrase from the list.

approximately   disembark   locate
~~personal electronic devices~~   place
proceed to   rear   requiring

1 **Cell phones, tablets, and laptops** may be used in flight mode during the flight. *personal electronic devices*

2 There are bathrooms at the front and at the **back** of the plane. _____

3 Our flight time today is **about** two and a half hours. _____

4 The crew will be passing through the cabin with ear phones for any passengers **needing** them. _____

5 Passengers to New York are asked to **go to** Gate 36 immediately. _____

6 Please check that you have all your belongings with you before you **leave the plane**. _____

7 We ask that you **put** bags and jackets under the seat in front of you. _____

8 Please take some time now to **find** your nearest emergency exit. _____

b (Circle) the correct word.

1 They booked first-class tickets, so they could use the *airport terminal /* (airline lounge) while waiting for their flight.

2 It didn't take long for me to check in my suitcase at the *baggage drop / security.*

3 The passengers were stopped at *customs / the check-in desk* for their bags to be checked.

4 I showed my boarding pass and ID at the *baggage claim / gate* and went to board my flight.

5 I didn't have a boarding pass, so I had to stand in line at the *check-in desk / customs* to get one.

6 We could see our plane on the *runway / gate* while we were waiting to board.

7 We parked as close as possible to the *airport terminal / airline lounge* because we were late.

8 The quickest way to find your flight is to look at the *departures board / runway.*

9 I was wearing boots, so I had to take them off at *security / the baggage drop.*

10 When I went to the *baggage claim / flight times*, I found that my suitcase hadn't arrived.

c Complete the sentences with a word from the list.

arrivals   ~~business class~~   cart   collect
delayed   first class   illegal goods   luggage

1 Companies usually pay for employees to travel *business class* _____.

2 If your suitcase has wheels, you don't need to use a _____.

3 There's usually a line of taxis waiting outside _____.

4 Passengers who are traveling _____ sit in the most comfortable seats on the plane.

5 You should always keep your _____ with you when you're in an airport.

6 Customs officers check travelers' bags to make sure they are not trying to bring _____ into the country.

7 It can sometimes take a long time to get out of the airport if you have to wait to _____ your bags from the baggage claim.

8 The departures board informs passengers whether a flight is on time, boarding, or _____.

d Complete the text.

Last year, I wanted to travel from Calgary to San Diego to visit a friend. I had booked an [1]int*ernational* fl*ight* from Calgary to Los Angeles and a [2]c_____ fl_____ from Los Angeles to San Diego. I printed my [3]b_____ p_____ the day before my flight, and I took it with me to the airport. I was able to go right to security in [4]D_____ because I only had a [5]c_____ b_____ – a small backpack. After [6]sc_____ my bag, they opened it and [7]ch_____ it to make sure I wasn't carrying any [8]l_____ or [9]sh_____ ob_____, like scissors. When I finally got my bag back, I looked at the [10]d_____ b_____ to see if my flight was already [11]b_____. I shouldn't have worried, because the flight was [12]d_____. The plane didn't [13]t_____ o_____ until two hours later. When I eventually arrived in Los Angeles, I was happy to see that my next flight was [14]o_____ t_____. However, just before we were due to [15]b_____, we were informed that the flight had been canceled – apparently, planes couldn't [16]l_____ in San Diego because of fog. In the end, I finished my journey by train, and I arrived in San Diego eight hours late!

e Complete the crossword.

Crossword (partially filled):
- 1 (across): A I S L E
- 4 (across): S _ T [ ] B _ T
- 5 (across): C _ _ N [ ] C _ W
- 6 (across): T _ R _ _ _ _ E
- 8 (across): J _ T [ ] L G
- 9 (across): D _ _ _ T _ C [ ] F _ _ _ T
- Down 2: L E ... L F
- Down 3: D ... T T F
- Down 7: R ... W E

ACROSS →

1 the passage between the rows of seats on a plane

4 a thing that you fasten around your body to hold you in your seat

5 the people whose job it is to take care of passengers on a plane

6 a series of sudden and violent changes in the direction that air is moving

8 the tired feeling that people often have after a long journey on a plane to a place where the local time is different

9 a flight between places within the same country

DOWN ↓

2 a flight that transports people over long distances, e.g., between two continents

3 a flight that goes from one place to another without stopping

7 a line of seats on a plane

f Circle a, b, or c.

1 I ____ abroad five or six times a year.
   a journey   **b travel**   c trip

2 I had a terrible ____ here – the flight was delayed, and then we had a lot of turbulence.
   a journey   b travel   c trip

3 Is Hannah back from her ____ to South America?
   a journey   b travel   c trip

4 We have to ____ 250 miles if we want to see my grandparents.
   a journey   b travel   c trip

5 My sister wants to go on a ____ around the world after she graduates from college.
   a journey   b travel   c trip

6 I went on a long train ____ across Canada last year.
   a journey   b travel   c trip

g Complete the phrasal verbs in the questions with a particle from the list.

---
in   off (x3)   on   out   up (x2)
---

1 Who **picked** you _up_____ from the airport the last time you traveled?

2 When do you usually **check** _____ for a flight?

3 Who usually **drops** you _____ at the airport?

4 Have you ever **filled** _____ an immigration form? If so, when?

5 What's the first thing you do when you **get** _____ a plane?

6 Have you ever **picked** _____ the wrong bag at the baggage claim?

7 Are you usually in a hurry to **get** _____ the plane? Why / Why not?

8 Do you ever feel nervous when a plane **takes** _____?

h Answer the questions in **g**.

1 _____

2 _____

3 _____

4 _____

5 _____

6 _____

7 _____

8 _____

Go online for more practice

2 GRAMMAR IN CONTEXT
so / such...that...

Circle the correct word.

1 Her suitcase was *so* / *so much* / *such* heavy that she couldn't pick it up.

2 We had *so* / *such* / *such* a long delay that we missed our connecting flight.

3 There were *so* / *so much* / *so many* people at the airport that there weren't any carts left.

4 We flew over *so* / *such* / *such* a beautiful countryside that I took some photos from the plane.

5 There was *so* / *so much* / *so many* rain that the road to the airport was flooded.

6 We were sitting in *so* / *so much* / *such* narrow seats on the plane that it was very uncomfortable.

7 The flight attendant spoke *so* / *so much* / *such* softly that I couldn't hear what she was saying.

3 GRAMMAR narrative tenses, past perfect continuous

a Circle the correct verb form. Check (✓) if both are correct.

1 Tim couldn't close his suitcase because he *had put* / *had been putting* too many clothes in it.

2 She *had worked* / *had been working* for the same airline for eight years before she was promoted. ✔

3 I was delighted when I found my passport. I *had looked* / *had been looking* for it for hours.

4 After I *had picked up* / *had been picking up* my luggage, I took a taxi to my hotel.

5 I *had sat* / *had been sitting* in departures for 20 minutes when I saw that my flight was boarding at a different gate.

6 They *had lived* / *had been living* in Brooklyn before they moved to Boston.

7 The passengers were angry because the airline *had canceled* / *had been canceling* their flight.

8 I was surprised when I was told that my suitcase was too big: I *had taken* / *had been taking* it for years without having to pay for it.

b Complete the text with the correct form of the verbs in parentheses.

My parents [1] *had never flown* (never fly) before, so they were very nervous when we [2] _____ (arrive) at Logan Airport to take our flight to Mexico. It [3] _____ (rain), so I [4] _____ (leave) them at the terminal building with instructions to get in line at the check-in desk while I [5] _____ (go) to park my car in the long-term parking lot. However, when I [6] _____ (get) to the check-in desk myself, they were nowhere in sight. I [7] _____ (look) for them everywhere until it suddenly occurred to me that it was possible they [8] _____ (already / check in) and they [9] _____ (wait) for me in the departure lounge. This was a real problem for me because I [10] _____ (give) my passport to my mother, so I couldn't check in. I [11] _____ (call) my parents on their cell phone and, fortunately, my mother answered. They [12] _____ (already / go) through to the departure lounge, and they [13] _____ (wait) for me for almost half an hour at the gate. Apparently, my mom [14] _____ (read) her book and my dad [15] _____ (do) a crossword. After we hung up, my mom found an understanding staff member who met me at the information desk with my passport!

c Write a paragraph about an air travel experience you have had. Use several different narrative tenses.

4 PRONUNCIATION irregular past forms, sentence rhythm

a Write the simple past of the verbs in the list next to the simple past verb that has the same pronunciation of the vowel sound.

~~catch~~ cut fly meet pay say sing stand tell wake

1 bought	*caught*	6 spoke	_____
2 rang	_____	7 sold	_____
3 made	_____	8 knew	_____
4 let	_____	9 could	_____
5 shut	_____	10 read	_____

b ◀ 3.1 Listen and check. Then listen again and repeat the simple past forms.

c ◀ 3.2 Listen and fill in the blanks in the anecdote.

We were on a [1] *flight* to **Tokyo**, and we'd been [2] _____ for about [3] _____ **hours**. I was **listening** to [4] _____, and my [5] _____ was **sleeping**, when [6] _____ we **heard** a **very loud** [7] _____. It [8] _____ as if an **engine** had **exploded**. The [9] _____ **didn't tell** us what had [10] _____ until **half** an **hour later**.

d ◀ 3.2 Listen again and practice reading the anecdote aloud with the right rhythm.

Go online for more practice

G the position of adverbs and adverbial phrases   **V** adverbs and adverbial phrases   **P** word stress and intonation

1 GRAMMAR the position of adverbs and adverbial phrases

a (Circle) the adverb or adverbial phrase that is different.

1	**time**	all day (indoors) soon tonight
2	**place**	here in fact in the park outside
3	**manner**	absolutely fluently rudely slowly
4	**degree**	a little almost hard very
5	**comment**	clearly fortunately obviously sometimes
6	**frequency**	always hardly ever usually right away

b Re-order the words to make sentences. Put the adverb in its usual position.

1 I / umbrella / an / had / luckily / taken
Luckily, I had taken an umbrella.

2 sick / hardly ever / daughter / is / my
_____.

3 parents / next year / are / his / retiring
_____.

4 boy / rude / teacher / was / to / the / extremely / his
_____.

5 dresses / my / stylishly / very / sister
_____.

6 is / Omar / apparently / divorced / getting
_____.

7 were / would / you / never / thought / I / have / 30
_____.

8 bandaged / was / by a nurse / his ankle / carefully
_____.

9 be / in five minutes / I'll / there
_____.

10 go / much / the / to / later / in / I / summer / bed
_____.

c In each sentence one of the highlighted adverbs or adverbial phrases is in the wrong position. Rewrite the sentences.

1 He usually immediately gets up when his alarm rings.
He usually gets up immediately when his alarm rings.

2 Although she studies a lot, she goes rarely to the library.
_____
_____

3 I crashed my new car unfortunately last week.
_____
_____

4 Ideally, we should leave tomorrow early.
_____
_____

5 I can understand a word hardly when people speak English quickly.
_____
_____

6 Hiro almost forgot yesterday his doctor's appointment.
_____
_____

7 She's angry incredibly because her husband came home late last night.
_____
_____

8 It surprisingly didn't rain at all while we were in London.
_____
_____

2 VOCABULARY adverbs and adverbial phrases

a Circle the correct word.

1 Ellie ate all her lunch, *ever / even* the vegetables!

2 I haven't seen Tyler *late / lately*, have you?

3 I can't stand most TV shows, *specially / especially* reality shows.

4 Dave *near / nearly* crashed his car, but he braked just in time.

5 Please don't tell me what happens because I haven't read the book *still / yet*.

6 I'm not going to Sam's party. I *hard / hardly* know him! He's your friend, not mine.

7 Do you *ever / even* wear jeans to work?

8 My grandparents don't live *near / nearly* here; they live about 30 miles away.

9 My father worked very *hard / hardly* all his life.

10 Alan's feet are so big that his shoes are *especially / specially* made for him.

11 My cousin is a doctor, and *right now / actually* she's working in Africa.

12 I can't wait to find out what happens *at the end / in the end* of this book.

13 I missed my bus because I got up *late / lately*.

14 We were thinking of going to the movies, but *at the end / in the end* we just went out for some coffee.

15 I thought the movie was going to be boring, but *actually / right now* I really enjoyed it.

16 I didn't finish the exam – I was *still / yet* writing when the teacher told us to stop.

b Complete the sentences with an adverb from the list that matches the definition in brackets.

---
apparently ~~basically~~ certainly eventually
gradually ideally in fact obviously
---

1 *Basically* (the main reason is), we don't have enough money to buy our own house.

2 _____ (in a perfect world), we'd each have our own room in the house, but that isn't possible.

3 That's _____ (without a doubt) the best lobster that I've ever eaten – it was delicious!

4 My sister is _____ (little by little) building a new life for herself after her divorce.

5 If you keep applying for jobs, you'll find one _____ (in the end).

6 I thought the meal was going to be expensive, but _____ (the truth is) it was very reasonable.

7 _____ (clearly), her son will move out when he gets a job, but for now he's living with her.

8 _____ (according to what I've heard), a lot of flights have been canceled because of the bad weather.

c Complete the stories with the correct adverbs from the lists.

HOODLUMS

~~aggressively~~ hardly ever luckily now

The young men walked [1] *aggressively* through the crowded shopping mall. They had their target in their sights and wouldn't stop until they had done what they had set out to do.
  [2] _____ she felt scared. She ran from the hooded gang, stopped, and was cornered.
  "Miss, you forgot your handbag."

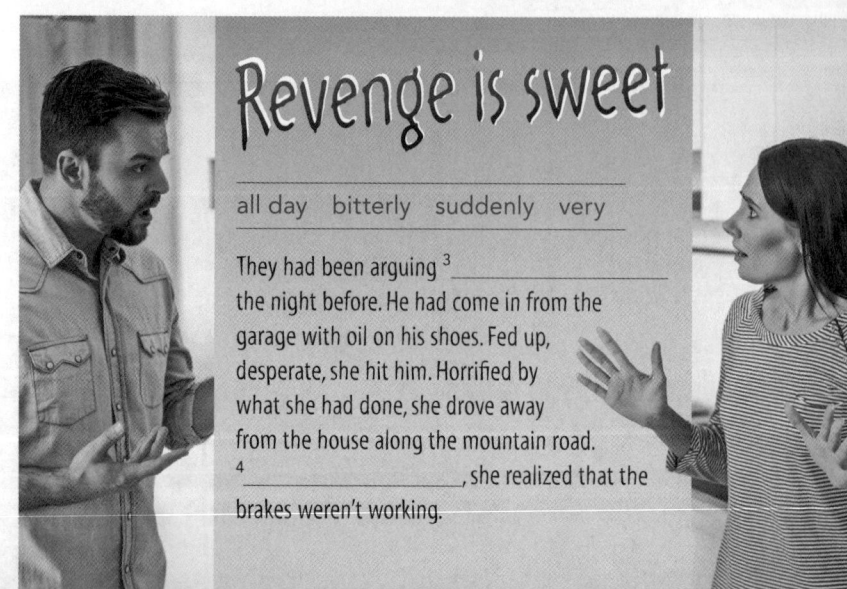

Revenge is sweet

---
all day bitterly suddenly very

They had been arguing [3] _____ the night before. He had come in from the garage with oil on his shoes. Fed up, desperate, she hit him. Horrified by what she had done, she drove away from the house along the mountain road.
  [4] _____, she realized that the brakes weren't working.

Go online for more practice

Generation

gap

always   angrily   extremely   unfortunately

He was worried. ⁵_____, since his wife's death, his teenage daughter had become ⁶_____ difficult. They had agreed 2:00 a.m. as the latest return time from clubs. Now it was 3:30. He prepared himself for confrontation as the door opened. "Dad," she shouted ⁷_____. "I've been frantic. You're late again."

The story of my life

actually   last week   normally   slightly

Stage one: Feel fat. Go on diet. Lose weight. Feel fabulous. Buy new clothes.

Stage two: Eat ⁸_____ but controlling intake. Look fabulous. New clothes ⁹_____ tight.

Stage three: Eat and drink normally (potatoes, bread, dessert, and soda). New clothes don't fit. Old clothes thrown away.

Back to stage one.

---

d Choose six adverbs or adverbial phrases from the list and write sentences that are true for you.

a lot   apparently   fluently   here   ideally   incredibly slowly   sometimes   tonight   usually

1 _____
2 _____
3 _____
4 _____
5 _____
6 _____

3 PRONUNCIATION word stress and intonation

a <u>Underline the stressed syllable in the adverbs in the list. Then put them in the correct column.

<u>ab</u>|so|lute|ly   ac|tu|a|ly   a|ppar|ent|ly   ba|si|ca|lly   de|fi|nite|ly e|ven|tual|ly   e|spe|cia|lly   fortu|nate|ly   gra|dua|lly   i|de|a|lly in|cre|di|bly   lu|cki|ly   ob|vi|ous|ly   un|fortu|nate|ly

Stress on first syllable	Stress on second syllable
absolutely	

b 🔊 3.3 Listen and check. Then listen again and repeat the adverbs.

c 🔊 3.4 Listen and complete the sentences.

1 I *absolutely* love Japanese food, *especially* sushi.
2 I thought Brad was single, but _____ he's _____.
3 We paid a lot for the tickets, but _____, the play was _____ boring.
4 That movie is _____ – even my husband cried at the end!
5 I _____ want to change my job, _____ for something better paid.
6 _____, Tina has been downsized, so she's moving back in with her _____.

d 🔊 3.4 Listen again and repeat the sentences. Copy the stress and intonation of the adverbs.

🔄 **Go online** for more practice   ✓ **Go online** to check your progress

2&3 Colloquial English Books

1 LOOKING AT LANGUAGE

Fill in the blanks to complete the conversations.

1 **A** Which book have you enjoyed reading recently?
  B *The Hunger Games.* A*lright*_____, it was written for teenagers, but I really liked it.

2 **A** How do you like that e-reader I gave you?
  B I was worried I wouldn't use it but, a_____, it's very handy.

3 **A** Do you know anything about Ken Follett's books?
  B I think they're s_____ o_____ thrillers, aren't they?

4 **A** Have you ever read a Charles Dickens novel in English?
  B No way! I m_____, it would be too hard, wouldn't it?

5 **A** Did you enjoy *Crime and Punishment*?
  B Yes, although it was a little bit, y_____ kn_____, depressing in places.

6 **A** What do you think of the writer Dan Brown?
  B W_____, he's not a great writer, but I enjoy his books.

2 VOCABULARY FROM THE INTERVIEW

Complete the sentences from the interview with Marion Pomeranc with a verb from the list.

brought ~~flow~~ go rules take

1 The words, the made-up words, the way the words *flow*_____ together and sound.
2 It just _____ me to a different place.
3 Kids like to _____ back, they like to become familiar with a character in the story.
4 _____ a trip to a publishing house.
5 Youth dominates, and kind of _____ the world a little bit.

3 THE CONVERSATION

Complete the sentences with two possible words or phrases from the list.

I mean kind of (x2) like sort of (x2) stuff things

1 You can just *kind of*_____ / *sort of*_____ lose yourself in this imaginary world.
2 I like science fiction and fantasy and _____ / _____ like that.
3 It's just something I _____ / _____ grew up with.
4 _____ / _____, it's something that I would recommend to my friends and family.

4 VOCABULARY FROM THE CONVERSATION

Replace the *italic* words with a word or phrase from the list.

a clue huge key to out of it ~~tough~~

1 It's really *difficult*. *tough*_____
2 I don't have *any idea*. _____
3 I feel a little *bit disconnected*. _____
4 It's *so big*. _____
5 That's the *critical thing about* any good book. _____

GRAMMAR & VOCABULARY

a Complete the sentences with the correct form of the **bold** word.

1 I don't agree with my brother's _____ views. He refuses to listen to other people's opinions. **MIND**

2 Your wrist is very _____ – I think you might have sprained it. **SWELL**

3 Andrea is taking antibiotics because she has a nasty throat _____. **INFECT**

4 Matt was _____ relieved when he found out he'd passed his driver's test. **INCREDIBLE**

5 My shoulders got sunburned because I was wearing a _____ dress. **SLEEVE**

6 She tends to wear clothes that are practical rather than _____. **FASHION**

7 There was a long line at _____ because only one of the scanning machines was working. **SECURE**

8 My dad's picking me up from the airport – he said he'd wait for me in _____. **ARRIVE**

9 We had some shelves _____ made for the space between the cabinet and the window. **SPECIAL**

10 Living on my own felt strange at first, but I'm _____ getting used to it. **GRADUAL**

b Read the article. Circle a, b, or c.

LUCKY ESCAPE AT TRABZON AIRPORT

Can you imagine how [1]____ if you were on a plane that slid off the runway when it landed? This is exactly what happened on a domestic flight in Turkey one evening in January 2019. The plane had [2]____ without incident from the capital, Ankara, and the flight had continued as usual. However, the pilot had difficulties as he [3]____ in Trabzon, in the northeastern part of the country. Freezing temperatures in the area [4]____ a thick layer of ice to form on the runway. The ice was [5]____ slippery that when the Boeing 737-800 landed, the wheels began to slide. The pilot tried to correct the mistake, but he [6]____. The plane slid off the tarmac and started going towards the cliffs above the Black Sea. [7]____, the wheels got stuck in the mud on the side of the cliffs, and the plane stopped before it reached the water. At the time, there were 168 people on board: 162 passengers, two pilots, and four cabin [8]____. Fortunately, they only had to wait 20 minutes for emergency services to arrive and help them get off. [9]____ were taken directly to the hospital, but they were all sent home within a very short time. Psychologists say it may take time for some of the passengers to [10]____ the shock.

	a	b	c
1	did you feel	you would feel	would you feel
2	dropped off	picked up	taken off
3	landed	had landed	was landing
4	caused	had caused	had been causing
5	so	so much	such
6	couldn't	hadn't	wasn't
7	Ideally	Luckily	Obviously
8	staff	attendants	crew
9	Injured	People injured	The injured
10	come around	get over	pass out

✓ **Go online** to check your progress

Stormy weather

G future perfect and future continuous   **V** the environment, weather   **P** vowel sounds

1 GRAMMAR future perfect and future continuous

a (Circle) the correct form.

1 Hopefully, we *will be saving / will have saved* enough money to go on vacation by the summer.

2 By this time tomorrow, *we will be traveling / we will have traveled* to Chicago – it's an eight-hour journey, so take something to do on the train.

3 I probably *won't have finished / won't be finishing* the report by Friday – can I give it to you on Monday morning?

4 Don't call between one and two o'clock because we *will have had / will be having* lunch.

5 We *will have had / will be having* five meetings by the end of today.

6 Jack *will be leaving / will have left* for Mexico on Saturday. I'm taking him to the airport.

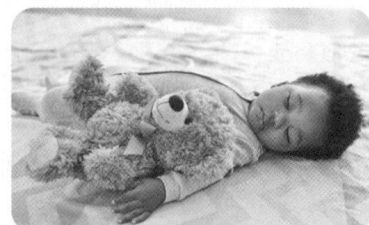

7 I won't see my children tonight – they *will be going / will have gone* to bed by the time I get home.

8 I've planned a surprise party for Alex – when we get to the restaurant, all her friends *will be waiting / will have waited* for her!

b Complete the sentences with the future perfect or future continuous form of the verb in parentheses.

1 By the end of this month, we*'ll have moved* (move) to our new house, so you can visit us.

2 By this time tomorrow, my parents _____ (fly) over the Pacific on their way to Tokyo.

3 My exams are in May, so I _____ (take) them all by June 1st.

4 Hopefully, you _____ (read) the book I lent you by the next time I see you.

5 If the game starts at 7:00 p.m., we _____ (play) until 8:45 at least.

6 In a year, they _____ (build) the new road, and we'll be able to get to work much quicker.

7 When do you think you _____ (finish) paying your mortgage?

8 Don't call me tomorrow morning because I _____ (attend) an important meeting.

9 It's been raining all morning, but hopefully it _____ (stop) by this afternoon.

10 _____ (you go) to the supermarket later?

c Write future perfect or future continuous questions.

1 when / you / take / your next vacation
When will you be taking your next vacation?

2 what / you / do / this time tomorrow
_____

3 what time / you / get up / tomorrow morning
_____

4 how much TV / you / watch / by the end of the week
_____

5 where / you go / next weekend
_____

6 when / you / finish / your English homework
_____

7 how many times / you / look at your phone / by the end of today?
_____

8 how many hours / you / spend / study English / by the end of the week
_____

d Answer the questions in **c**.

1 _____
_____

2 _____
_____

3 _____
_____

4 _____
_____

5 _____
_____

6 _____
_____

7 _____
_____

8 _____
_____

2 VOCABULARY the weather

a Circle the word that is different.

1 below zero   cold   cool   (mild)
2 damp   drizzling   drought   humid
3 boiling   freezing   hot   scorching
4 breeze   chilly   hurricane   windy
5 changeable   fog   mist   smog
6 pouring   showers   warm   wet

b Complete the sentences.

1 We're having a h_eat wave_____. It isn't usually so hot at this time of year.
2 Many drivers had to spend the night in their vehicles after they were caught in the bl_____ and their cars got stuck in the snow.
3 People say that there may be a fl_____ if the river continues rising.
4 In some areas there was h_____. The balls of ice were enormous!
5 Last night there was a violent storm and the sound of th_____ woke me up.
6 The government wants us to save water because of the dr_____.
7 In India, the m_____ season usually lasts until October. The rain can be very heavy.
8 The l_____ lit up the sky during the thunderstorm.
9 Hundreds of trees blew down in the h_____, and several buildings were damaged.

c Match 1–9 to a–i.

1 Everyone is hoping for clear   _c_
2 They said the weather will be changeable,   ____
3 There were so few sunny   ____
4 The forecast is for heavy   ____
5 Planes can't take off in this thick   ____
6 Driving will be dangerous this morning because of the icy   ____
7 Most parts of the tri-state area will enjoy bright   ____
8 Many trees were blown down by strong   ____
9 We hope the weather will be more settled   ____

a roads, so drivers should take care.
b next week – we're going on a cruise.
c ~~skies so that they can see the solar eclipse.~~
d sunshine today, and it will be warm.
e rain, so the barbecue has been canceled.
f winds during last night's storm.
g so I'm taking my sunglasses and an umbrella.
h fog, so several flights have been canceled.
i periods that we didn't spend much time at the beach.

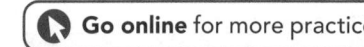 **Go online** for more practice

d Complete the paragraphs with the words in each list.

freezing heavy icy strong

January is one of the coldest months in New York State. The temperature sometimes drops to 32°F, so it's [1] _freezing_ outside, and the roads are [2] _____. There are often [3] _____ winds and [4] _____ rain or snow; during some storms, sleet may fall instead of rain.

breeze changeable mild showers sunny

In April, it isn't as cold, and some days can be very [5] _____ – around 60°F. There are often rain [6] _____, with [7] _____ periods between them because the weather is very [8] _____. There's often a [9] _____, which can sometimes be very cool.

bright cool hail settled warm

In June, the weather still isn't [10] _____, and it continues to change a lot: one minute there's [11] _____ sunshine, and the next it rains. Thunderstorms often move through, producing heavy rain and sometimes even balls of [12] _____. In general, it's [13] _____ during the day – around 70°F – but it can get [14] _____ in the evenings, so you need a light jacket.

chilly clear drizzle damp mist rain

By October, the temperature starts to fall again, and it can be very [15] _____ outside – only 50°F or 55°F. Some mornings start out with [16] _____ in the mountains and near the water, while on others there are [17] _____ skies and you can see for a long way. Towards the end of the fall, the weather can be rather [18] _____: sometimes just a light [19] _____ and other times pouring [20] _____.

e Write a paragraph about the weather in your country in January, April, July, and October.

3 PRONUNCIATION vowel sounds

a (Circle) the word with a different sound.

1	tree	breeze freezing (great) heat wave
2	boot	cool flood monsoon typhoon
3	bike	bright icy lightning mist
4	owl	blow drought shower towel
5	fish	blizzard drizzling chilly mild
6	up	humid summer sunny thunder
7	ear	clear here wear zero
8	egg	heat heavy sweat weather
9	horse	scorching storm warm world
10	phone	although below cloudy snow

b ◖4.1 Listen and check. Then listen again and repeat the words.

Go online for more practice

4B A risky business

G zero and first conditionals, future time clauses   **V** expressions with *take*   **P** linked phrases

1 GRAMMAR zero and first conditionals, future time clauses

a Complete the sentences with a verb from the list. Decide if they are zero conditional or first conditional sentences. Write **0** (zero) or **1** (first).

are   cooks   doesn't answer   doesn't come
~~don't get~~   eat   'll stay   won't move

1 Plants die if they *don't get*_____ enough water. _0_
2 If you _____ too many calories, you gain weight. ____
3 I _____ at a friend's house tonight if I miss the last train. ____
4 My sister _____ her phone if she's watching a movie on TV. ____
5 Some dogs bite if they _____ scared. ____
6 If we don't sell our house, we _____. ____
7 If Justin _____ dinner tonight, Karen will be delighted. ____
8 If the bus _____ soon, I'll take a taxi. ____

b Complete the sentences with the correct form of the verb in parentheses.

1 *Bring*_____ your swimsuit if you want to use the pool. (bring)
2 If my wife _____ home before 7:30, she gets caught in rush hour traffic. (not leave)
3 It's raining. You'll get wet if you _____ an umbrella with you. (not take)
4 Don't interrupt Emily if she _____. (study)
5 If you _____ 18 or over, you can vote in a general election. (be)
6 If you can't take me to the airport, I _____ a friend. (ask)
7 If you _____ Jodi Picoult's new book yet, I'll buy you a copy for your birthday. (not read)
8 If I _____ eight hours of sleep, I always feel awful the next day. (not get)

c Complete the second sentence so that it means the same as the first sentence. Use a time expression from the list and no more than two other words.

~~after~~   as soon as   before   if   in case   unless   until   when

1 I'll do Pilates, and then I'll take a shower.
  I'll take a shower *after I do*_____ Pilates.
2 My boyfriend will arrive at his hotel. He'll call me immediately.
  My boyfriend will call me _____ at his hotel.
3 We'll arrive in time for lunch if the traffic isn't bad.
  We'll arrive in time for lunch _____ is bad.
4 I'm going to call my husband. He might forget his doctor's appointment.
  I'm going to call my husband _____ his doctor's appointment.
5 Sarah is going to pack her suitcase. Then she'll go to bed.
  Sarah is going to pack her suitcase _____ to bed.
6 We'll wait for you to get home. Then we'll have dinner.
  We won't have dinner _____ home.
7 I might be late tonight, so don't wait up for me.
  Don't wait up for me _____ late tonight.
8 I'll go to New York and I'll stay with some friends.
  I'll stay with some friends _____ to New York.

d Complete the sentences about you.

1 I'll have dinner after _____ .

2 I'll buy a new car as soon as _____ .

3 I won't go to bed tonight until _____ .

4 I'll go shopping before _____ .

5 I might go out later if _____ .

6 I won't move to a new house unless _____ .

7 I'll finish my English homework now, in case _____ .

8 I'll retire when _____ .

2 PRONUNCIATION linked phrases

a 🔊 4.2 Listen and complete the sentences.

1 *First of all* _____, let's see how much money we have.

2 I didn't really want to go, but it was _____ the end.

3 Dress professionally, _____, don't be late.

4 _____ world, everyone would have a roof over their head.

5 Don't disturb me _____ important.

6 I'll call you _____ I get home.

7 _____ I'm concerned, there's nothing more to say.

8 It was _____ experience that I don't really want to think about it.

b 🔊 4.2 Listen again and repeat the words. Copy the rhythm.

3 VOCABULARY expressions with *take*

a Match the sentence halves.

1 Grandparents often **take care of** children ___*i*___
2 Don't **take a risk**, ____
3 Try to **take** all the factors **into account** ____
4 If you get an interesting job opportunity, ____
5 There's a new restaurant opening in my neighborhood; ____
6 If you want to be involved in the protest, ____
7 Most people **take pity on** people ____
8 The Olympics **take place** every four years; ____
9 Please don't hurry; ____

a if you think something bad might happen.
b they're always held in a different country.
c they're looking to **take on** a new cook as well as several food servers.
d **take advantage of** it.
e who are homeless.
f before you make a decision.
g you can **take your time**.
h you can **take part in** the demonstration.
i when their parents can't look after them.

⬤ **Go online** for more practice

b Complete the sentences with the **bold** phrases in **a**.

1 We didn't _take_ the rush hour traffic _into account_ , so we almost missed our flight.

2 Why don't we _____ the sunny weather and go to the beach?

3 My children love drama, so they always _____ the school play.

4 This report doesn't need to be finished today – you can _____.

5 The pilot decided to _____ and try to land the plane on the river.

6 I always _____ my elderly neighbor when he's sick. I visit him every day to check if he needs anything.

7 Most music festivals _____ in the summer months when it's more likely to be sunny.

8 Could you _____ my cat while I'm on vacation?

9 Don't mind Charlie. He doesn't _____ other children very quickly.

c Match the **bold** phrasal verbs in 1–8 to definitions a–h.

1 When was the last time someone **took** you **out** for dinner? __d__

2 Who was the last person you **took to** immediately? ____

3 Do you **take** your shoes **off** as soon as you go into your house? ____

4 Do you **take your time** doing your English homework? ____

5 In what ways do you **take after** your parents? ____

6 How often do you **take** the trash **out**? ____

7 Have you ever watched the planes **take off** and land at an airport? ____

8 If you could **take up** a new activity, what would it be? ____

a to leave the ground and begin to fly

b to use as much time as you need without hurrying

c to remove a piece of clothing

d to take somebody to a place and pay for them

e to start liking somebody

f to learn or start to do something, especially for pleasure

g to remove something from inside, e.g., a house

h to look or behave like

d Answer the questions in **c** about you.

1 _____
_____

2 _____
_____

3 _____
_____

4 _____
_____

5 _____
_____

6 _____
_____

7 _____
_____

8 _____
_____

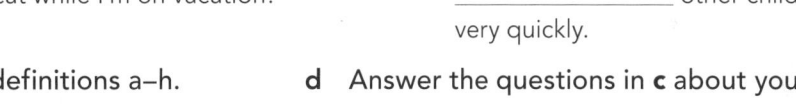

Go online for more practice   Go online to check your progress

5A I'm a survivor

Adventure is just bad planning.
*Explorer Roald Amundsen,
first man to reach the South Pole*

G unreal conditionals **V** feelings **P** word stress in three- or four-syllable adjectives

1 VOCABULARY & PRONUNCIATION
feelings; word stress

a How would you feel in these situations? Complete the crossword.

```
¹O  F  F  E  N  D  E  ²D
                     U        T
              ⁴P           D
    ⁵H
         ⁶G              ⁷F
         ⁸R              D
                         ▓
 ⁹M              E
                 D       P
    K
      ¹⁰L        Y
```

ACROSS →
1 Someone told you that your new hairstyle makes you look old.
3 You have an argument with your best friend, and they say they never want to see you again.
4 Your daughter won a painting competition.
8 You think you lost your house keys, and then you find them at the bottom of your bag.
9 You're camping, it's raining, and everything is soaking wet.
10 All your friends are on vacation, and you have nobody to talk to.

DOWN ↓
2 You weren't offered a job after you went to the interview.
5 You're studying abroad and you're missing your family.
6 It's pouring rain and a friend offers to drive you to your home.
7 Your flight has already been delayed three times, and then it's canceled.

b Replace the underlined words with an adjective from the list.

astonished   bewildered   delighted
desperate   devastated   horrified
overwhelmed   stunned   ~~thrilled~~

1 They're <u>very excited</u> to be traveling around South America after saving for so long.
   thrilled

2 When you buy a new phone, it's easy to get <u>very confused</u> by all the different options and contracts.
   _____

3 People were <u>extremely shocked and disgusted</u> when they heard about the terrorist attack.
   _____

4 Andy was <u>amazed</u> when his parents gave him a car for his birthday.
   _____

5 She was <u>so surprised that she couldn't react</u> when she saw the fire damage.
   _____

6 Olivia was <u>incredibly pleased</u> when she got promoted.
   _____

7 My brother was <u>extremely upset</u> when his wife left him.
   _____

8 The soldier's wife was <u>so happy that she didn't know how to react</u> when her husband suddenly arrived home after six months away.
   _____

9 The climbers were <u>losing hope</u>. It was getting dark, snowing heavily, and they couldn't figure out a way down the mountain.
   _____

c Complete the sentences a word from the list.

couldn't believe his eyes   ~~down~~   jumping for joy
scared stiff   sick and tired of   worn out

1 My sister was a little bit _down_ after her interview exam went badly.

2 I'm _____ always having to tell my husband to clean up.

3 Javier was _____ when he saw a big dog running towards him.

4 I couldn't sleep on the flight from New York. I'm absolutely _____ today.

5 Ahmet _____ when his favorite celebrity retweeted him on Twitter.

6 I was _____ when I got accepted to my top choice college.

d Underline the stressed syllable in the adjectives in the list. Then put them in the correct column.

a|sto|nished   be|wil|dered   de|ligh|ted   de|spe|rate
de|va|sta|ted   dis|a|ppoin|ted   grate|ful   home|sick
horr|i|fied   lone|ly   mi|se|ra|ble   o|ffen|ded   o|ver|whelmed
re|lieved   up|set

Stress on first syllable	Stress on second syllable	Stress on third syllable
	astonished	

e ◖5.1 Listen and check. Then listen again and repeat the adjectives. Copy the rhythm.

f Choose six feelings in **d** that you have experienced yourself. Write a sentence about when you experienced each feeling.

1 _____
_____

2 _____
_____

3 _____
_____

4 _____
_____

5 _____
_____

6 _____
_____

2 GRAMMAR unreal conditionals

a Circle the correct form.

1 Our boss *was / would be* more popular if he didn't take himself so seriously.

2 I would have gotten cold if I *didn't take / hadn't taken* a jacket.

3 You *hadn't have / wouldn't have* sprained your ankle if you'd been looking where you were going.

4 I'd really miss you if you *went / would go* to live in Seoul.

5 Vicki *had / would have* more friends if she didn't complain all the time.

6 I *had been / would have been* really disappointed if I hadn't got the job.

7 He *didn't be able to / wouldn't be able to* afford a new car if he wasn't living with his parents.

8 We wouldn't have gone to Thailand in June if we *knew / had known* it was the monsoon season.

9 Jacob wouldn't be so stressed if he *had / would have* a more understanding boss.

10 We wouldn't have gotten lost if we *had stayed / would have stayed* on the path.

b Complete the second and third conditional sentences.

1 We don't go away on weekends because we don't have much free time.
   If we had more free time, *we'd go away on weekends.*

2 There wasn't much snow, so we didn't make a snowman.
   If there had been more snow, _____.

3 I didn't know the water was so cold, so I jumped in.
   I wouldn't have jumped in if _____.

4 He doesn't pass his driver's test because he gets so nervous.
   He would pass his driver's test if _____.

5 We missed the last bus because we left the party too late.
   If we'd left the party earlier, _____.

6 You get sunburned because you don't use enough sunscreen.
   If you used more sunscreen, _____.

7 They hadn't read the book, so they didn't really understand the movie.
   They would have understood the movie if _____.

8 I don't earn a lot of money, so I can't buy my own house.
   If I earned more money, _____.

c Complete the text with the correct form of the verbs in parentheses.

What would **you** do if…?

¹ *Would you be* (you / be) prepared if there was an emergency on your plane?
Think about the last time you flew. Did you pay attention to the safety demonstration? If ² _____ (you / not go) to sleep, you would have heard the flight attendant explain the location of the emergency exits. This information is vital. If there had been a fire, ³ _____ (you / have) only about 90 seconds to get off the plane.

It's unlikely that there will be an emergency on your flight, but if there is, the most important thing is to be ready.

d Continue the second and third conditional sentences about you.

1 If my parents were billionaires, _____
   _____.

2 If I could travel anywhere in the world, _____
   _____.

3 If I spoke perfect English, _____
   _____.

4 If I had been born in a different country, _____
   _____.

5 If I had lived in the 19th century, _____
   _____.

6 If I had gotten up earlier this morning, _____
   _____.

Would you know what to do if ⁴ _____ (you / get lost) in the mountains?
The number one survival tip is to stop walking and wait to be rescued. In research done in Canada, however, only two out of 800 lost people actually did this. If ⁵ _____ (the others / not keep) walking, a search and rescue team would have found them much more quickly. If they had waited in an open space, ⁶ _____ (a helicopter / see) them immediately.

The most important thing when you go hiking is to tell someone where you are going, so that you can be rescued if anything goes wrong.

What ⁷ _____ (you / do) if you heard somebody in your house in the middle of the night?
Imagine you woke up and there was someone in the kitchen. The worst thing you could do is confront the intruder because he might have a weapon.

Instead you should lock yourself and your family inside a bedroom or the bathroom and call the police. Of course, this would be impossible if ⁸ _____ (you / not have) your cell phone with you. So you should always keep your phone fully charged by the side of your bed.

  Go online for more practice

5B Wish you were here

Never look back unless you are planning to go that way.
Henry David Thoreau, author, poet, and philosopher

G *wish* for the present / future, *wish* for past regrets | **V** expressing feelings with verbs or *-ed* / *-ing* adjectives | **P** sentence rhythm and intonation

1 GRAMMAR *wish* for the present / future

a Match 1–8 to a–h.

1 I hardly ever see my boyfriend. _d_
2 My new clothes are always disappearing. ____
3 The weekend has flown by. ____
4 My brother's playing loud music again. ____
5 I'd love to study abroad. ____
6 The kitchen is a mess. ____
7 My neighbors' car is always outside my house. ____
8 Public transportation is terrible around here. ____

a I wish I had a car.
b I wish he would wear headphones.
c I wish you would wash the dishes.
d ~~I wish he didn't work on weekends.~~
e I wish my sister wouldn't borrow them.
f I wish I spoke better English.
g I wish they wouldn't park there.
h I wish it wasn't Monday tomorrow.

b Read the sentences in **a**. Decide if they show that the speaker would like something to be different, or that he / she is annoyed about something? Complete the chart.

speaker wants something to be different	speaker is annoyed about something
1	

c Complete the sentences with *wish* + simple past or *wish* + *would*.

1 My ex-boyfriend is driving me crazy! He calls me every day.
  I wish *my ex-boyfriend wouldn't call me every day.*
2 It's a difficult decision, and I don't know what to do.
  I wish *I knew what to do.*
3 My boss really annoys me. She shouts all the time.
  I wish _____.
4 I didn't get the job because I can't drive.
  I wish _____.
5 I'm fed up with my brother using my computer.
  I wish _____.
6 I can't stand it when my son stays in bed all morning.
  I wish _____.
7 I want to speak to Dan, but I don't have his phone number.
  I wish _____.
8 I hate it when you leave the bathroom a mess.
  I wish _____.
9 I'd love to go away this weekend, but I have to work.
  I wish _____.
10 I have lots of books, but I don't have time to read.
  I wish _____.

d What would you like to be different? What annoys you? Write six sentences with *wish* + simple past or *wish* + *would*.

1 _____
2 _____
3 _____
4 _____
5 _____
6 _____

35

2 VOCABULARY expressing feelings with verbs or *-ed* / *-ing* adjectives

a Complete the sentences with an adjective or a verb made from the word in parentheses.

1 It really *infuriates* me when people talk loudly on their cell phones on trains. (infuriate)
2 Looking after my sister's three small children is _____ for my parents. (exhaust)
3 Ethan was so _____ when he failed his driver's test. (disappoint)
4 My boyfriend is scared of flying. The idea of getting on a plane _____ him. (terrify)
5 My son is a terrible loser. Not winning something really _____ him. (frustrate)
6 You should try the new Asian restaurant on Main Street. The food is _____. (amaze)
7 I was so _____ when my phone rang during the meeting. (embarrass)
8 His first visit to the theater _____ him to take up acting. (inspire)
9 I find the New York City subway system very _____. I've gotten on the wrong train many times. (confuse)
10 We were _____ that so many people came to our party. (thrill)

b Complete the chart.

verb	*-ed* adjective	other adjective
1 delight	*delighted*	*delightful*
2 impress		
3 offend		
4 scare		
5 stress		

c Complete the sentences with an adjective from **b**.

1 He was *offended* when the teacher suggested he might have cheated on the exam.
2 We were _____ when we received a surprise visit from some old friends.
3 She gave such an _____ performance in the movie that I think she might win an Oscar.
4 I'm _____ with your English. You speak really well.
5 The bridge started to move from side to side as we were crossing, which was very _____.
6 She's a little _____ right now because she's taking care of her sister's children as well as her own.
7 I found his sexist comments very _____.
8 Joe's _____ of small spaces – he never uses the elevator.
9 My nieces are _____ – they're very sweet, and they're always making things for me.
10 My boss is good at staying calm in _____ situations.

3 VOCABULARY FROM READING

Complete the sentences with the correct word from a pair in the list.

---
afraid / fear   angry / anger   brave / bravery
encouraging / encouragement
enthusiastic / enthusiasm   ~~excited~~ / excitement
honest / honesty   sorry / sorrow

1 My nephew's very *excited* about his birthday tomorrow.
2 I wish my boyfriend was more _____ – I've caught him telling lies recently.
3 She raised her voice in _____ when she saw the children behaving so badly.
4 I'm not very _____ about the party – I don't really want to go.
5 I wish I had written to my uncle to express my _____ about the death of my aunt.
6 My art teacher is very _____ about my work – she thinks I'm pretty good.
7 The soldier received a medal for his _____ – he had risked his life to protect his unit.
8 The child was shaking with _____ after being chased by a big dog.

Go online for more practice

4 GRAMMAR *wish* for past regrets

a Match 1–8 to a–h. Then complete a–h with the past perfect form of a verb from the list. Use contractions.

bring ~~leave~~ not eat not fall not shout
not spend study wear

1 I'm going to be late.   _e_
2 It's colder than I thought today.   ____
3 I feel sick.   ____
4 I failed half of my exams.   ____
5 My leg hurts.   ____
6 I upset my little sister.   ____
7 It's pouring rain.   ____
8 I don't have a lot of money left.   ____

a I wish I _____ an umbrella.
b I wish I _____ so much on that meal last night.
c I wish I _____ harder.
d I wish I _____ at her this morning.
e ~~I wish I'd left~~ _____ ~~home earlier.~~
f I wish I _____ off my bike.
g I wish I _____ a warmer sweater.
h I wish I _____ that seafood.

b Read the situation and write sentences beginning with *I wish* + past perfect.

1 I took the train to work, but it broke down and I was late.
   I wish I hadn't taken the train to work.

2 I left my cell phone on my desk, and now it isn't there.
   _____.

3 I didn't give my boss the report on time, and now he's annoyed with me.
   _____.

4 My girlfriend didn't call me last night, and now I'm worried.
   _____.

5 My friend didn't invite me to her wedding, and now I'm upset.
   _____.

6 We lost our last basketball game, so we won't be playing in the final.
   _____.

7 I was rude to my mother, and now she's offended.
   _____.

8 My son woke me up in the middle of the night, and I couldn't get back to sleep again.
   _____.

5 PRONUNCIATION sentence rhythm and intonation

a ◉5.2 Listen and complete the sentences.

1 I wish I'd _applied_ for _____.
2 I wish you'd _____ at the _____.
3 I wish I _____ these _____.
4 I wish we'd _____ at _____.
5 I wish you _____ me _____.
6 I wish we _____ on the _____.

b ◉5.2 Listen again and repeat the sentences. Copy the <u>rhy</u>thm and intonation.

 Go online for more practice   ✓ Go online to check your progress

1 LOOKING AT LANGUAGE

Circle the correct comment adverb in the conversations.

1 A How do you recycle your organic waste?
  B We don't. *Ideally / Obviously / Unfortunately*, it's impossible to do that where we live.

2 A Who's in charge of emptying the trash cans in your house?
  B *Amazingly / Gradually / Sadly*, my teenage son always takes the trash out.

3 A How do you dispose of old electrical devices?
  B *Actually / Eventually / Unfortunately*, it's not usually a problem because I rarely buy new ones.

4 A What kind of things do you recycle?
  B *Amazingly / Apparently / Basically*, we try to recycle as much as we can.

5 A Can you see any problems with recycling?
  B *Actually / Anyway / Obviously*, you need four different recycling bins in the kitchen, but apart from that, it's easy.

6 A What happened to that beautiful old vase you had?
  B *Generally / Sadly / Strangely* it broke, so we had to throw it away.

7 A Have they come to empty the recycling bins yet?
  B No, they haven't. They always come on Mondays, but *basically / in fact / strangely* they haven't come today.

2 VOCABULARY FROM THE INTERVIEW

Complete the sentences from the interview with a phrase from the list.

worn out   ~~ended up~~   falling apart   pretty much
off the hook   for the sake

1 We *ended up* _____ filming in 11 countries.
2 He wears his sweaters until they're _____.
3 He keeps his cars until they're _____.
4 He can make _____ anything look beautiful.
5 I don't like to blame one person because that lets us _____.
6 We shouldn't buy new things _____ of it.

3 THE CONVERSATION

Circle the best response.

1 There are plastic bottles that you can eat when you've finished the water.
  a Yes, isn't that awful?
  b Oh wow!
2 There's more plastic in the sea by weight than fish.
  a That sounds pretty cool.
  b I mean, that's so depressing, isn't it?
3 I can't believe how much plastic there is.
  a Yes, it's very scary!
  b Oh wow!
4 They've found plastic in the Marianna Trench.
  a Yes, isn't that awful?
  b I think that's just so amazing.
5 They've found bacteria that have evolved to digest nylon plastic.
  a Its really awful, actually.
  b That's amazing!

4 VOCABULARY FROM THE CONVERSATION

Complete the sentences with a word from the list.

day   ~~doubt~~   hilarious   involved   taste

1 I would without a *doubt* _____ recommend this book.
2 I couldn't stop laughing; it was just _____.
3 I'd really like to get _____ with animals.
4 Reading biographies affects my life and just how I act day-to-_____.
5 But it comes down to _____, doesn't it?

GRAMMAR & VOCABULARY

a Complete the second sentence so that it means the same as the first sentence. Write 2–5 words. Use the word in parentheses.

1 I met John when we were students. (known)

   I've known John since _____ we were students.

2 My son's girlfriend is from Turkey; she's young and interesting. (Turkish)

   My son is going out with an _____
   _____ woman.

3 There's no doubt you'll save money if you sell your car. (certainly)

   You _____
   _____ if you sell your car.

4 It started to rain two hours after we started walking. (had)

   We _____
   _____ two hours when it started to rain.

5 My flight to Las Vegas leaves at 11:00 tomorrow and arrives at 12:15. (flying)

   At 12:00 tomorrow, I _____
   _____ to Las Vegas.

6 My classes end in May next year. (will)

   My classes _____
   _____ by June.

7 If the concert isn't sold out, I'll get you a ticket. (unless)

   I'll get you a ticket for the concert _____
   _____.

8 I got a cold because I went out with wet hair. (have)

   If I hadn't gone out with wet hair, _____
   _____ a cold.

9 It annoys me when you don't listen to me. (wish)

   I _____
   listen to me.

10 I regret not visiting The Louvre when I was in Paris. (visited)

   I _____
   The Louvre when I was in Paris.

b Read the article. Circle a, b, or c.

Thai cave rescue
Boys survive nine days trapped underground

In the summer of 2018, 12 teenage soccer players became trapped deep inside a cave in Thailand with the coach who was taking [1]_____ them. They had entered the cave to celebrate one of the boy's birthdays, but [2]_____ rains had flooded the cave, so they couldn't get out. For nine days, the boys and the coach were sitting in complete darkness, which must have been very [3]_____. They managed to survive by drinking the water dripping from the cave walls and by eating the snacks they had bought for the birthday party. [4]_____, the 25-year-old coach, Ekapol Chantawong, refused to eat any of the food so that the boys would have more for themselves. He helped them stay calm by teaching them meditation. When divers [5]_____ found the boys, they were [6]_____ to see that all the boys were still alive. They were also astonished to find that the boys didn't seem particularly [7]_____ by their experience. The rescue team, on the other hand, was in a race against time to get the boys out of the cave before the [8]_____ rains began. They had also noticed that the level of oxygen in the cave was dropping. The rescue operation took [9]_____ over three days and resulted in all 13 boys being taken safely out of the cave. There was a moment of [10]_____, however, when diver Saman Gunan died while he was helping to bring air tanks through the tunnels for the boys.

	a		b		c
1	after		care of		pity on
2	hard		heavy		strong
3	scare		scared		scary
4	Apparently		Basically		Certainly
5	lately		eventually		gradually
6	bewildered		grateful		relieved
7	stress		stressed		stressful
8	blizzard		hurricane		monsoon
9	part		place		risks
10	anger		sorrow		loss

✓ **Go online** to check your progress

6A Night night

G *used to, be used to, get used to*   **V** sleep   **P** /s/ and /z/

1 GRAMMAR *used to, be used to, get used to*

a (Circle) the correct word.

1 Before my sister had children, she used to (sleep)/ *sleeping* for eight hours every night.
2 When we moved to Thailand from the US, we weren't used to *drive / driving* on the left.
3 Chris got divorced last year, but he soon got used to *live / living* on his own.
4 I *used to / use to* know her well, but we lost touch after college.
5 Max *would / used to* have a beard when he was a student.
6 My parents are slowly getting used to *be / being* retired.
7 My new job is exhausting. I'm not used to *work / working* so hard.
8 Did you use to *play / playing* a musical instrument in school?
9 When Lily was a teenager, she *used to / was used to* eat pizza almost every day.
10 When I was a child, my mom *would / was used to* read to me every night before I went to bed.

b Complete the sentences with the base form or gerund of a verb from the list.

be   cook   go   have   live
~~play~~   study   take care of   talk   use

1 I used to *play* basketball well when I was a teenager.
2 Neil is a chef, so he's used to _____ for a lot of people.
3 My sister has gotten used to _____ in New York now, though she didn't like it at first.
4 My grandparents didn't use to _____ a phone when they were first married.
5 I don't think I could get used to _____ a total vegetarian.
6 When I was a child, my whole family would _____ for a walk every Sunday afternoon.
7 Emma has never lived on her own before, so she isn't used to _____ herself.
8 Did you use to _____ with music on when you were in college?
9 Ben will have to get used to _____ public transportation when he starts his new job.
10 People used to _____ to friends in person, not online.

c Complete the second sentence so that it has a similar meaning to the first sentence. Use a form of *used to, be used to,* or *get used to* and a verb.

1 Stephen wasn't so affectionate in the past.
Stephen *didn't use to be* _____ so affectionate.
2 Has working at night become less of a problem now?
Have you _____ at night?
3 Rob couldn't sleep because he doesn't usually sleep on a sofa.
Rob couldn't sleep because he _____ on a sofa.
4 Chloe wore her sister's clothes when she was a child.
Chloe _____ her sister's clothes when she was a child.
5 We have adapted to living in the country very quickly.
We have _____ in the country very quickly.
6 In the past, Main Street was full of stores, but now many have closed down.
Main Street _____ full of stores, but now many have closed down.
7 They still don't know how to use the new computer system – they keep making mistakes.
They haven't _____ the new computer system yet.
8 I don't usually have breakfast so early.
I'm _____ breakfast so early.

d Write about things you *used to / didn't use to* do as a child and things you're *used to / you've gotten used to* doing these days.

When I was a child...

_____
_____
_____
_____
_____
_____
_____
_____

These days...

_____
_____
_____
_____
_____
_____
_____

2 PRONUNCIATION /s/ and /z/

a 🔊 6.1 Listen and complete the sentences.

1 Terry is *used to working* at night.
2 We've gotten _____ in a tiny apartment.
3 Antibiotics are drugs that are _____ infections.
4 I never _____ problems sleeping.
5 I _____ a room, but now I have my own.
6 A cart is a small vehicle that is _____ things.

b 🔊 6.1 Listen again. In which sentences is *used* pronounced /yuzd/ and in which is it pronounced /yust/?

c 🔊 6.1 Listen and repeat the sentences. Copy the rhythm.

d Write the words in the correct column.

bus buzz cause course eyes ice loose lose peace peas place plays price prize race raise

 ![snake] 1 **s**nake	 ![zebra] 2 **z**ebra
bus	*buzz*

e 🔊 6.2 Listen and check. Then listen again and repeat the words.

🔴 **Go online** for more practice

3 VOCABULARY sleep

a Complete the sentences.

1 I tried not to y_awn_____, but I was tired and I couldn't help it.
2 We were cold in bed, so we got a bl_____ from the closet.
3 She has to wear earplugs at night because her husband sn_____.
4 I was feeling sl_____, so I went to bed.
5 My grandmother takes sl_____ p_____ to help her to sleep.
6 If I get up early, I try to take a n_____ after lunch.
7 It was warm and wonderful in the bed because there was a nice thick c_____ on it.
8 I was so tired that I fell asleep as soon as I put my head on the p_____.
9 Eric has in_____ – he just can't sleep at night.
10 It's very hot in the summer where we live, so we only have a sh_____ on the bed.

b Match 1–9 to a–i.

1 Our neighbors often keep ___f___
2 My husband is a light ____
3 I didn't hear last night's storm – I always sleep ____
4 Before I travel, I often have ____
5 On weekdays, I always set ____
6 Our children were ____
7 Apparently, I used to sleepwalk when I was a child; ____
8 I often fall ____
9 If you oversleep, ____

a nightmares about missing my flight.
b fast asleep by the time we got home.
c you'll miss your bus.
d the alarm for seven o'clock.
e sleeper – the slightest noise wakes him up.
f ~~us awake with their loud music.~~
g asleep during long plane trips.
h like a log.
i one day my mother found me in the yard!

c Complete the questions with the correct form of a verb from the list.

be   fall   have   keep   oversleep
set   ~~sleep~~   sleepwalk

1 _Are_____ you a light sleeper, or do you _sleep_____ like a log? Why?
2 Do you ever _____ nightmares? What about?
3 Do you wake up on your own, or do you need to _____ an alarm?
4 When was the last time you _____? What time did you wake up?
5 How long does it usually take you to _____ asleep?
6 Do you know anyone who _____? If so, where do they usually go?
7 What sometimes _____ you awake?
8 When was the last time you _____ fast asleep and something or someone woke you up?

d Answer the questions in c about you.

1 _____
_____
2 _____
_____
3 _____
_____
4 _____
_____
5 _____
_____
6 _____
_____
7 _____
_____
8 _____
_____

Go online for more practice

6B Music to my ears

Music expresses that which cannot be put into words and that which cannot remain silent.
Victor Hugo, poet, novelist, and dramatist

G gerunds and infinitives **V** music **P** words from other languages

1 GRAMMAR gerunds and infinitives

a Circle a, b, or c.

1 Mia learned ____ the guitar when she was a teenager.
   a play   **b** (to play)   **c** playing

2 I don't mind ____ if you tell me which way to go.
   a drive   **b** to drive   **c** driving

3 I should ____ to some of their songs before I go to the concert.
   a listen   **b** to listen   **c** listening

4 Our teacher makes us ____ a lot of homework.
   a do   **b** to do   **c** doing

5 Tom's doctor suggested ____ a specialist about his back.
   a see   **b** to see   **c** seeing

6 We'd like ____ now because we're leaving early tomorrow.
   a pay   **b** to pay   **c** paying

7 My father is very overprotective. He doesn't let me ____ with my friends on the weekends.
   a go out   **b** to go out   **c** going out

8 The man denied ____ the laptop from my bag.
   a steal   **b** to steal   **c** stealing

9 Kim expects ____ her test scores on Friday.
   a get   **b** to get   **c** getting

10 I've given up ____ to the gym. It was too boring.
   a go   **b** to go   **c** going

11 I can't imagine ____ at 5:30 every morning.
   a get up   **b** to get up   **c** getting up

12 My son managed ____ his driver's test even though he was really nervous.
   a pass   **b** to pass   **c** passing

b Complete the sentences with the infinitive or gerund of the verb in parentheses.

1 I remembered *to buy* _____ milk, but I forgot to buy some bread! (buy)

2 If you can't sleep at night, try _____ for a while. (read)

3 My sister is trying _____ a new job – she doesn't get along with her boss. (find)

4 We need _____ a plumber because the shower's broken. (call)

5 That shirt needs _____ if you want to wear it tonight. (iron)

6 Laura forgot _____ her mother a birthday card. (send)

7 I'll never forget _____ my best friend for the first time. (meet)

8 I remember _____ the apple tree when I was a child. (climb)

c Complete the questions with the infinitive or gerund of a verb from the list.

add ~~download~~ go learn listen to see take want

1 What's the first song or album you remember _downloading_?
2 Which song always makes you __________ to dance?
3 Which artist or band would you most like __________ in concert?
4 Have you ever tried __________ an instrument? Which one?
5 Are there any songs you like right now that you want __________ to your playlist?
6 What kind of music do you avoid __________ if you can?
7 Have you ever forgotten __________ your tickets to a concert? If so, what happened?
8 Would you rather __________ to a small concert or a large music festival? Why?

d Answer the questions in **c** about you.

1 ______________________________
2 ______________________________
3 ______________________________
4 ______________________________
5 ______________________________
6 ______________________________
7 ______________________________
8 ______________________________

2 VOCABULARY & PRONUNCIATION
music; words from other languages

a Complete the crossword.

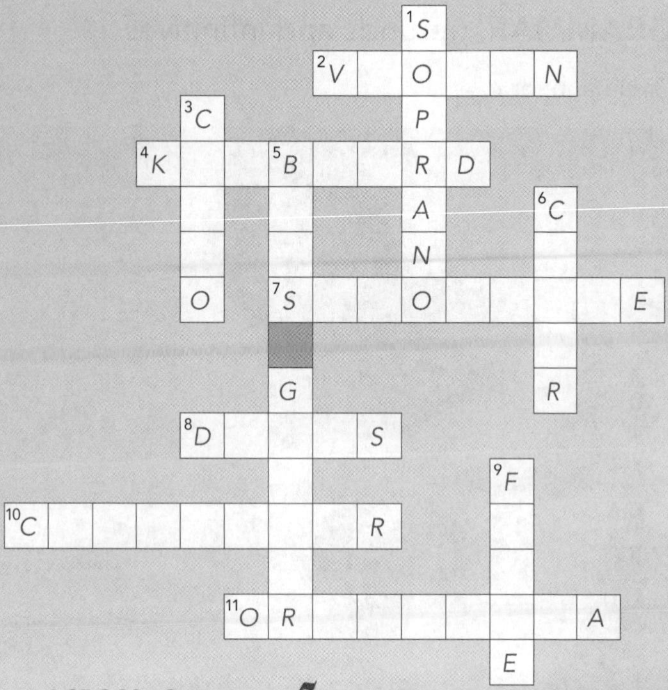

DOWN ↓

1

3

5

6

9

ACROSS →

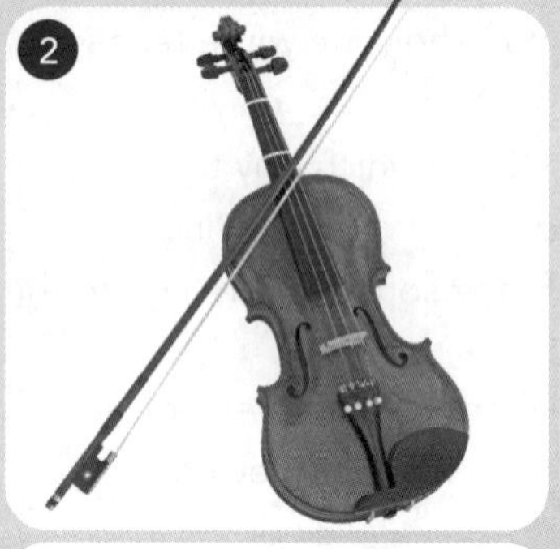
2

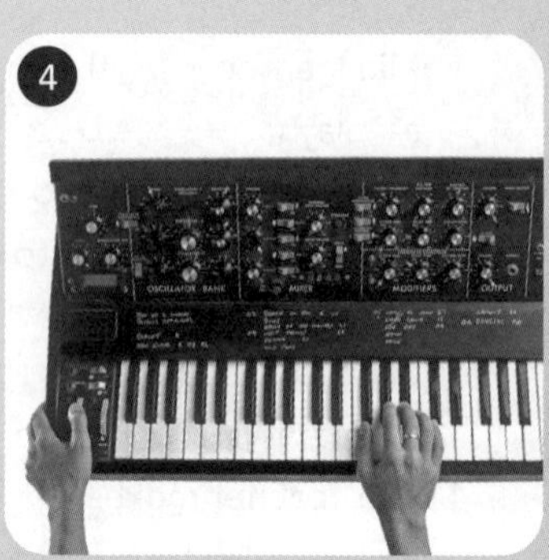
4

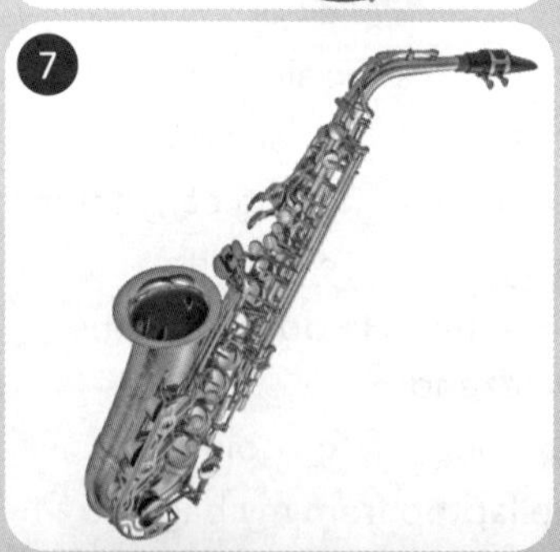
7

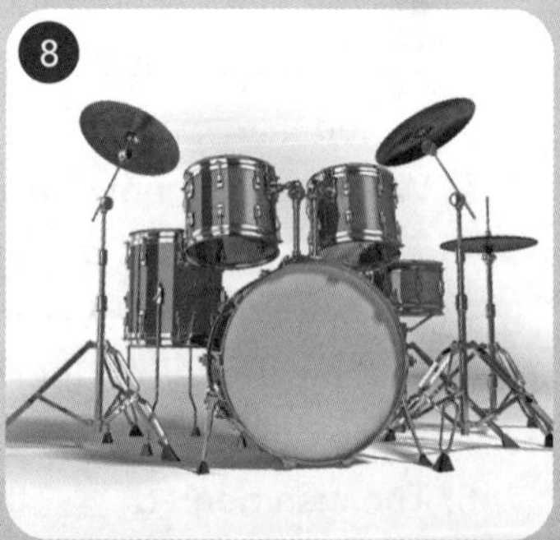
8

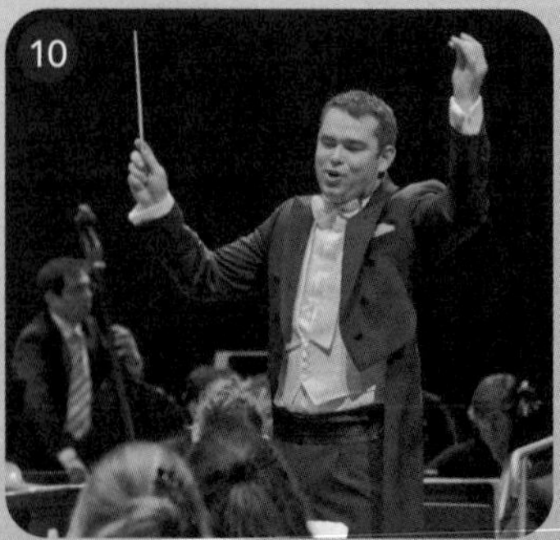
10

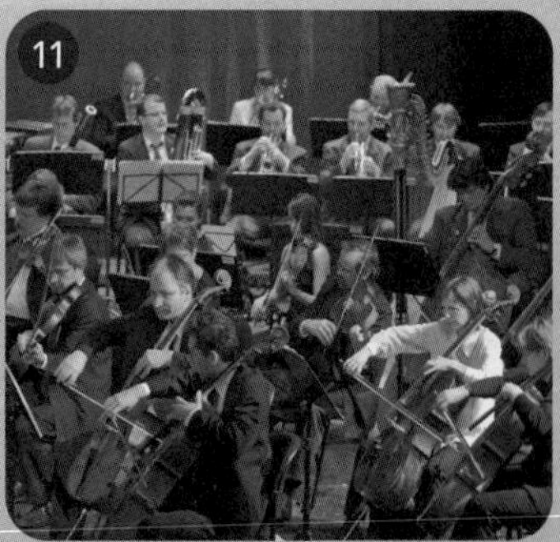
11

 Go online for more practice

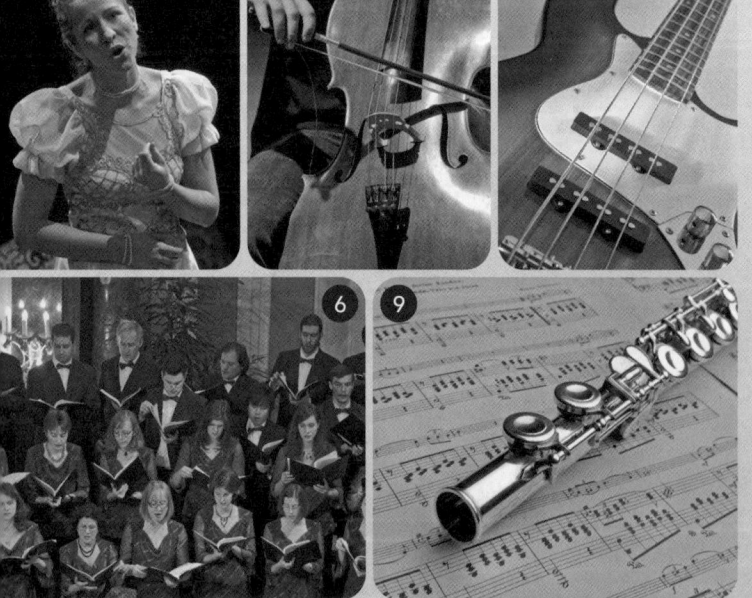

b Match the English words borrowed from other languages to the definitions.

~~ballet~~ chorus concerto encore genre
mezzo-soprano rhythm symphony

1 a style of dancing that tells a story with music but without words *ballet*
2 a long piece of music for a large orchestra, usually in three or four parts _____
3 a short, extra performance at the end of a concert _____
4 a singing voice with a range between soprano and alto
   _____
5 part of a song that is sung after each verse _____
6 a strong, regular, repeated pattern of sounds _____
7 a piece of music for an orchestra and one instrument playing a solo _____
8 a particular type or style of, e.g., music _____

c Underline the stressed syllable in the words in the list. Then put them in the correct column.

~~bal|let~~ ce|llo chor|us con|cer|to con|duc|tor en|core
gen|re gui|tar key|board or|che|stra rhy|thm
sax|o|phone so|pra|no sym|pho|ny vi|o|lin

Stress on first syllable	Stress on second syllable	Stress on third syllable
	ballet	

d 🔊6.3 Listen and check. Then listen again and repeat the words.

e (Circle) the word with a different sound.

keys	chess	shower	keys
1	2	3	4
choir	cappu**cc**ino	**ch**auffeur	bou**qu**et
(**ch**ili)	**c**ello	**ch**ef	en**c**ore
or**ch**estra	con**c**erto	**ch**ic	fian**c**é
psy**ch**ology	ma**cch**iato	**ch**orus	hypo**ch**ondriac

f 🔊6.4 Listen and check. Then listen again and repeat the words.

g 🔊6.5 Listen and complete the sentences.

1 The *barista* brought me my *croissant*.
2 The _____ is ruined by the _____.
3 A lot of _____ took _____ of the movie star.
4 The technician gave the _____ a _____.
5 The dancers in that _____ had a natural sense of _____.

h 🔊6.5 Listen again and repeat the sentences. Copy the rhythm.

Go online for more practice   Go online to check your progress

7A Let's not argue

My parents had only one argument in 45 years. It lasted 43 years.
Cathy Ladman, US comedian

G past modals: *must have, etc., would rather* | **V** verbs often confused | **P** weak form of *have*

1 GRAMMAR past modals: *must have*, etc.

a Match the sentences to the responses.

1 Ryan's phone was turned off. __c__
2 Stacey can't find her gloves. ____
3 Emma didn't make her bed this morning. ____
4 I was surprised that Tony didn't come to the party. ____
5 Leo just bought a brand new Porsche. ____
6 I'm pretty sure I saw Isabel at the gym today. ____
7 I'm not sure where Millie is. ____
8 My dad was downsized from his job when we were kids. ____

a It can't have been her – she's on vacation in Hawaii.
b She may have left them in her car.
c I think he might have been at the movies.
d He must have paid a fortune for it.
e She could have gone to a friend's house.
f She might not have had time.
g He couldn't have been very happy about that.
h He must have had something else to do.

b Complete the sentences with *must have, might have, might not have,* or *can't have* and the verb in parentheses.

1 You *must have been* so happy when you passed your driver's test – it was your first time, wasn't it? (be)
2 I'm not sure where Mark is, but he _____ home. He wasn't feeling well this morning. (go)
3 You _____ my parents at the supermarket. They're away on vacation. (see)
4 I don't know why my grandmother didn't open the door, but I guess she _____ the doorbell. (hear)
5 The "For Sale" sign is still up outside their house. They _____ yet. (move)
6 I don't understand how the accident happened, but the driver _____ asleep. (fall)
7 Those boys look really guilty. They _____ something wrong. (do)
8 Jin hasn't replied to my email. It's possible that she _____ it yet. (read)

c Write the next sentence using the words given.

1 My brother isn't talking to me.
  I / should / shout at him
  I shouldn't have shouted at him.
2 We're running out of gas.
  we / ought / fill up at the last gas station.
  _____
3 Someone has taken Ben's smartphone.
  he / should / leave it on his desk
  _____
4 You won't be able to walk in those shoes.
  you / should / buy such high heels
  _____
5 I had a nightmare last night.
  I / should / stay up to watch that horror movie
  _____
6 Your cousins look really scruffy.
  they / ought / dress up for the wedding
  _____
7 My alarm clock isn't working.
  it / should / go off at 7:30
  _____
8 Jessie missed her train.
  she / should / take a taxi to the train station
  _____

d Look at the photo. What do you think happened? What do you think the bike rider did wrong? Use *must*, *might / may / could*, or *can't / couldn't* to make deductions, and *should have / ought to have* to express criticism. Use the words in the list or your own ideas.

be / more careful   break / bike   ~~fall off / bike~~
hit / head   hurt / leg   ride / so fast   sprain / ankle
wear / protection

1 *She must have fallen off her bike.*
2 _____
3 _____
4 _____
5 _____
6 _____
7 _____
8 _____

2 PRONUNCIATION weak form of *have*

a ▶)7.1 Listen and write the sentences with either *have* or *of*.

1 *I cried at the end of the movie* .
2 _____ .
3 _____ ?
4 _____ .
5 _____ ?
6 _____ .

b ▶)7.1 Listen again and repeat the sentences. Copy the rhythm.

c ▶)7.2 Listen and complete the sentences.

1 They're taking Steve to the hospital. He might have *broken* a *bone* .

2 Diana isn't here yet. She can't have _____ my _____ .

3 It was only a joke. She shouldn't have _____ so _____ .

4 This restaurant's packed. We should have _____ a _____ .

5 I didn't hear the phone. I must have _____ .

6 Becky and Chen haven't come to the party. They may have _____ about it.

d ▶)7.2 Listen again and repeat the second sentences. Copy the rhythm.

3 GRAMMAR IN CONTEXT *would rather*

Rewrite the sentences using *would rather*.

1 I'd prefer it if you didn't post photos of me on Facebook.
I'*d rather you didn't post photos of me on Facebook* .

2 I don't really want to cook tonight, if you don't mind.
I _____ .

3 What do you want to do: stay in or go out?
What _____ ?

4 I'd prefer it if we took a taxi home, if that's OK with you.
I _____ .

5 I'd prefer to see that movie at the movie theater than on TV.
I _____ .

6 I'd prefer to sit by the window than next to the aisle.
I _____ .

🔵 **Go online** for more practice

4 VOCABULARY verbs often confused

a Complete the sentences with the correct **bold** verb.

1 **wish / hope**

   I _wish_ we had enough money to buy a bigger house.

2 **mind / matter**

   I don't _____ where we go. The important thing is to go on a vacation.

3 **avoid / prevent**

   My daughter will do anything to _____ doing housework. She's really lazy.

4 **remember / remind**

   _____ me to send my dad a card. It's his birthday next week.

5 **argue / discuss**

   My boyfriend and I often _____ about his friends. I really don't like them.

6 **lend / borrow**

   Could I _____ your phone charger? I left mine at home.

7 **notice / realize**

   I didn't _____ what the thief was wearing. It was too dark.

8 **beat / win**

   Our soccer team managed to _____ the game 1–0.

9 **expect / wait**

   I'll _____ outside while you see the doctor.

10 **raise / rise**

   Please _____ your hand if you have any questions.

11 **advise / warn**

   My uncle asked me to _____ him which laptop he should get.

12 **deny / refuse**

   I _____ to lend Austin anymore money. He never pays me back!

13 **lay / lie**

   All I want to do when I'm on vacation is _____ on the beach and sunbathe.

14 **rob / steal**

   Don't leave your phone on the table – somebody might _____ it.

b Complete the sentences with the simple past form of a verb from the pairs in the list.

advise / warn   argue / discuss   avoid / prevent
beat / win   deny / refuse   expect / wait   lay / lie
lend / borrow   mind / matter   notice / realize
raise / rise   ~~remember / remind~~   rob / steal   wish / hope

1 When I got to my car, I suddenly _remembered_ that the keys were in my other bag.

2 My parents _____ me the money to buy a new car, but I have to pay them back.

3 Canada _____ the US 3–2.

4 Two men _____ me while I was walking home. They got away with my bag and phone.

5 My colleague _____ taking my scissors, but I saw them later on his desk.

6 Last year we just _____ on the beach all day when we were on vacation.

7 House prices _____ last month for the first time this year.

8 At the meeting we _____ the possibility of working together.

9 The police officer's action _____ anybody from getting hurt.

10 I _____ our team to lose, but in the end they won.

11 At first, she didn't think it _____ that her husband traveled a lot, but eventually she got fed up with it.

12 The moment I heard her voice on the phone, I _____ something was wrong.

13 The tour guide _____ us that the area was dangerous at night.

14 We _____ the weather would be good for the picnic, but unfortunately it rained.

Go online for more practice

G verbs of the senses   **V** the body   **P** silent consonants

1 GRAMMAR verbs of the senses

a Circle the correct form.

1 Your skin *feels / feels like* dry. You need to use some hand cream.

2 Ken's sweating. He *looks / looks as if* he's been running.

3 We need to take out the trash. The kitchen *smells / smells like* terrible.

4 I'm not sure what's in this curry, but it *tastes like / tastes as if* chicken.

5 It *sounds / sounds as though* Tina has finally gotten up. I can hear her moving around.

6 Come in and sit by the fire. Your hands *feel like / feel as if* ice!

7 This soup *tastes / tastes as if* you put a lot of garlic in it.

8 You *seem / seem like* happy today. Did you get some good news?

9 I don't feel like *go / going out* tonight. Let's stay in and watch a movie.

10 You *sound / sound like* your mother when you talk like that.

b Complete the sentences with *look / feel / smell / sound / taste / seem* + adjective, *like* or *as if* where necessary.

1 My skin _feels_____ much softer since I've been using a new face cream.

2 What's that noise? It _____ thunder.

3 Ellen's boyfriend _____ a model – he's tall and incredibly good-looking.

4 Have you turned off the stove? It _____ something's burning.

5 This salad _____ horrible – it's really salty.

6 This swimming pool _____ it's heated. The water is very warm!

7 Your voice _____ strange. Do you have a sore throat?

8 Is anything the matter? You _____ a little distant today.

9 That aftershave _____ gas – I'm not sure if I like it.

10 Martha's hair is really messy. She _____ she's just gotten out of bed.

c Complete the description of the thing in photo 1 with *looks, smells, feels,* or *tastes*. Then write descriptions of the things in photos 2–4 using verbs of the senses.

1 a cake

2 garlic

3 blue cheese

4 a Siamese cat

1 It's a kind of food. It _looks_____ a little like bread. It _____ hot and kind of soft at first, but it gets harder on the outside when it's cold. It _____ delicious when it comes out of the oven, and it _____ even better when you eat it.

2 _____
_____
_____
_____
_____

3 _____
_____
_____
_____
_____

4 _____
_____
_____
_____
_____

2 VOCABULARY the body

a Complete the crossword.

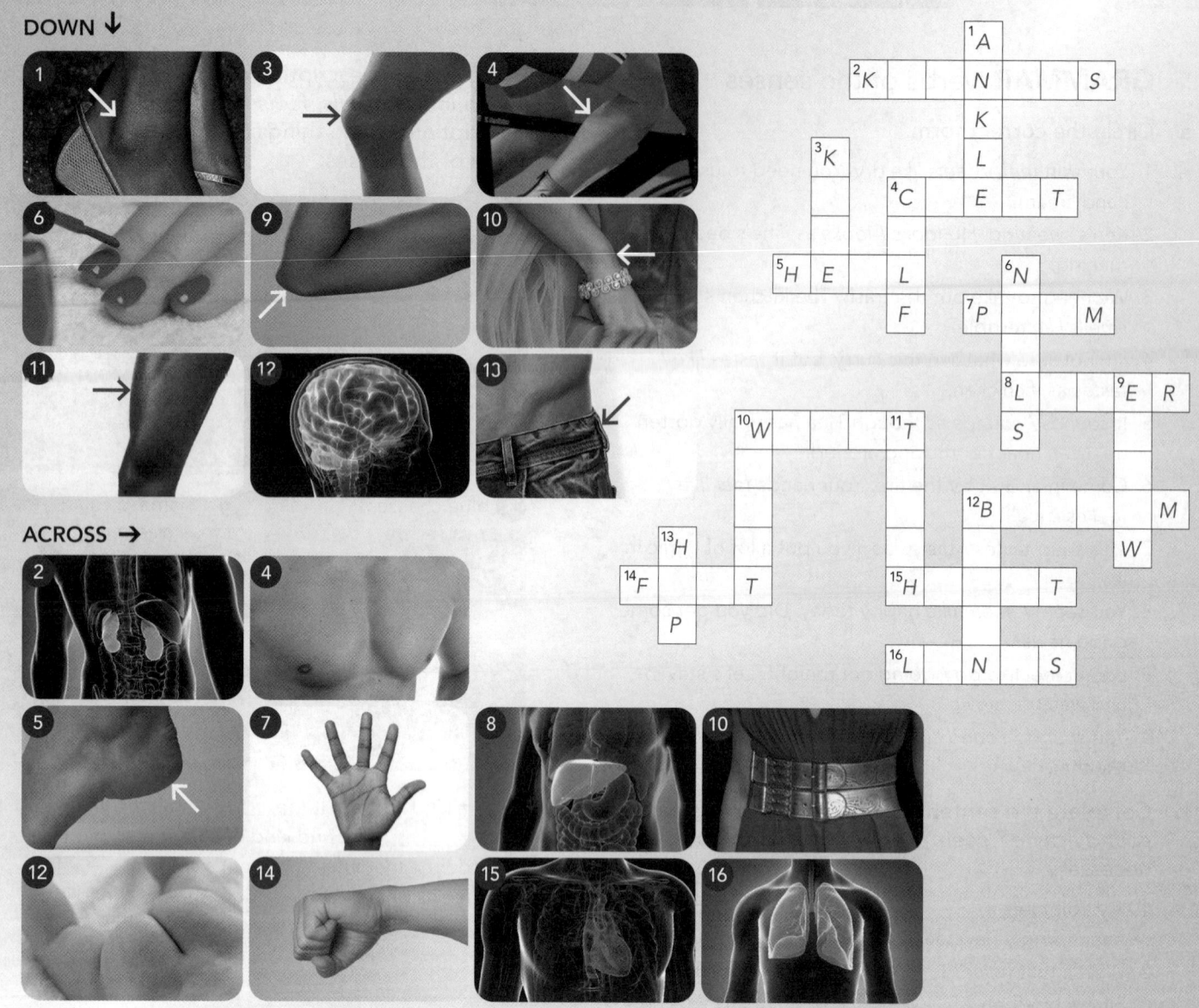

DOWN ↓

ACROSS →

b Match 1–13 to a–m.

1	Can you touch	_h_	a your nose.
2	When I asked if she'd passed, she shook	____	b my hand as we walked down the road.
3	I always brush	____	c her head sadly.
4	Adam shrugged	____	d his arms and stood watching me.
5	Here's a tissue so you can blow	____	e my thumb when I was a baby.
6	I used to suck	____	f his nails when he's nervous.
7	Jessie combed	____	g her hair and put on her jacket to go out.
8	She went into the room and shook	____	h ~~your toes?~~
9	Remember to brush	____	i his shoulders and said he didn't know.
10	When I told my boss, she raised	____	j your hair once you've washed it.
11	My boyfriend bites	____	k hands with the interviewer.
12	He folded	____	l her eyebrows in surprise.
13	My niece held	____	m my teeth after every meal.

🔵 **Go online** for more practice

c Complete the sentences with the simple past form of a verb from the list.

chew   frown   hug   kneel   point   scratch
~~stare~~   stretch   wave   wink   yawn

1 The children *stared*_____ at the ice cream in the store window.
2 Anna _____ her children and gave them each a kiss before she left the house.
3 He _____ as he read the letter – it can't have been good news.
4 We _____ each mouthful to make it last because we didn't know when we'd be eating again.
5 He got up and _____ to try and wake himself up.
6 The police officer _____ on the ground to examine the footprints.
7 I don't speak French, so I just _____ at the dessert I wanted.
8 My friend _____ at me when he saw me getting off the train.
9 My dad _____ at my daughter to show he wasn't being serious.
10 The baby _____ twice and then fell asleep.
11 Rami _____ the insect bites on his legs and made them bleed.

3 VOCABULARY FROM READING

Complete the sentences.

1 It's a con*tradiction*___ to say that you're friends with somebody but you don't trust them.
2 Don't l_____ to me – I need to know the truth.
3 The best way to de_____ a lie is by watching a person's body language.
4 I'm not a very good l_____, so I generally tell the truth.
5 The present was supposed to be a secret, but his wife g_____ it a_____.
6 People often use de_____ to make money or get something they want.

4 PRONUNCIATION
silent consonants

a ~~Cross out~~ the silent consonants in the words. Use the phonetics to help you.

1 ~~w~~rist   /rɪst/
2 thumb   /θʌm/
3 kneel   /nil/
4 palm   /pɑm/
5 muscle   /ˈmʌsl/
6 whistle   /ˈwɪsl/
7 honest   /ˈɑnəst/
8 fasten   /ˈfæsn/
9 aisle   /aɪl/
10 design   /dɪˈzaɪn/
11 whole   /hoʊl/

b 🔊 7.3 Listen and check. Then listen again and repeat the words.

c Look at the phonetics. Write the word.

1 /ˈkæsl/   *castle*_____
2 /huz/   _____
3 /daʊt/   _____
4 /ˈfɔrən/   _____
5 /rɔŋ/   _____
6 /kɑm/   _____
7 /naɪf/   _____
8 /ˈsɪzərz/   _____
9 /ˈrɪŋkl/   _____
10 /ˈaɪlənd/   _____
11 /wʌt/   _____
12 /ˈplʌmər/   _____

d 🔊 7.4 Listen and check. Then listen again and repeat the words.

e 🔊 7.5 Listen and complete the sentences.

1 They spent the *whole*_____ meeting discussing the new project.
2 I wish I had been more _____ about how I felt.
3 I don't know anyone who likes the _____ of the new shopping mall.
4 I'm so busy that I _____ I'll have time to get to the grocery store today.
5 I found a key, but I don't know _____ it is.
6 She looked surprisingly _____ after the accident.

( ) **Go online** for more practice   ( ) **Go online** to check your progress

1 LOOKING AT LANGUAGE

Complete the modifiers in the sentences.

1 The actors were utt*erly*_____ exhausted when the play was over.
2 The plot left the audience feeling com_____ bewildered.
3 As far as I'm concerned, the movie was tre_____ overrated.
4 So far, reviews of the play have been over_____ positive.
5 Mozart was an extra_____ talented musician.
6 The director was ab_____ delighted to receive the award.
7 All of the characters were wearing fan_____ original costumes.

2 VOCABULARY FROM THE INTERVIEW

Match the words from the interview to the definitions.

1 box office   *c*
2 rehearsal   ____
3 character   ____
4 auditorium   ____
5 scene   ____

a the place where an incident in real life or fiction occurs or occurred
b a practice or trial performance of a play or other work for later public performance
c a place at a theater, movie theater, etc., where tickets are bought or reserved
d a person in a novel, play, or movie
e the part of a theater, concert hall, or other public building in which the audience sits

3 THE CONVERSATION

Match the beginnings 1–6 to endings a–f.

1 That's a difficult question. __*d*__
2 I think it's difficult to say ____
3 But if you go to a live event, you participate, don't you, ____
4 If you're sitting, let's say, ____
5 I've been to plenty of live music events – concerts and festivals and things, you know, ____
6 That's intriguing, isn't it, ____

a high up or with a slightly obstructed view…
b because you're part of it.
c the difference between the two…
d I love going to the cinema…
e if it's better or worse…
f around the country, and I love them.

4 VOCABULARY FROM THE CONVERSATION

Complete the sentences and phrases with a word from the list.

| bouncing   certain   factors   flashy   soft |

1 watching a big *flashy*_____ superhero movie
2 a big _____ spot for the theater
3 It has a _____ magic to it.
4 You're part of it because they're _____ off you.
5 It depends on other _____.

GRAMMAR & VOCABULARY

a Complete the sentences with the correct form of the **bold** word.

1 My sister-in-law is rather _____-_____; she has a very high opinion of herself. **HEAD**

2 The boys were wearing _____ tops, so you couldn't see their faces. **HOOD**

3 _____, there's nothing we can do about the current situation; it's up to the politicians. **BASIC**

4 The weather forecasters said the weather will be _____, so take an umbrella in case it rains later. **CHANGE**

5 Toby's moving to a new house this week, which is a little bit _____. **STRESS**

6 The town hall is an _____ building in the center of town. **IMPRESS**

7 I _____ this morning, so I was late for work. **SLEEP**

8 The sound of the rain on the roof kept me _____ last night. **WAKE**

9 I _____ in bed for hours last night trying to get to sleep. **LIE**

10 Mirga is a famous _____ who has worked with orchestras all over the world. **CONDUCT**

b Read the article. Circle a, b, or c.

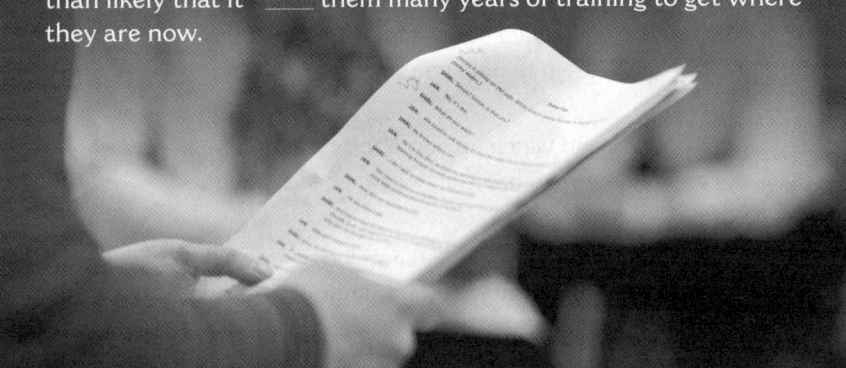

So you want to be an actor?

Many people think that acting ¹___ easy. They believe it's just a question of memorizing lines and delivering them in front of the camera. "If I could remember words, I ²___ be an actor, too," they say. Yet none of them would expect to become a professional singer overnight. In general, most people think that becoming a ³___ requires far more training than appearing on-screen.

In fact, it takes just as much training to be a good actor ⁴___ it does to become an opera singer. The difference is that an actor has to learn ⁵___ naturally so that the audience doesn't ⁶___ that he or she is acting. According to the famous teacher Stanford Meisner, "Acting is doing things truthfully under imaginary circumstances."

If a person ⁷___ to become a successful actor, he or she has to learn how to bring a script to life. From the moment he or she receives the pages, an actor will ⁸___ for action in the lines in order to make choices about his or her performance. The words are the writer's, but it's the actor who creates a believable character to express them.

In conclusion, it is impossible to wake up one morning and spontaneously decide to go out and get an acting job. The naturalness of an actor's performance might make you ⁹___ that anyone who can read or speak can be one. However, it's more than likely that it ¹⁰___ them many years of training to get where they are now.

	a		b		c
1	looks		looks like		looks as if
2	can		could		will be able to
3	concerto		soprano		symphony
4	as		like		than
5	perform		performing		to perform
6	advise		deny		realize
7	had wanted		wanted		wants
8	be looking		have looked		to look
9	think		thinking		to think
10	had taken		has been taking		has taken

✓ **Go online** to check your progress

No one truly knows a nation until one has been inside its jails.
Nelson Mandela

G the passive (all forms); *have something done; it is said that…, he is thought to…, etc.* **V** crime and punishment **P** the letter *u*

1 VOCABULARY crime and punishment

a Complete the text with the words in the list.

~~be burglarized~~ break into burglar burglary steal

I never thought that my apartment would
¹*be burglarized* because I live on the third floor.
But one day, I came home to find that the lock on my
front door was broken. When I called the police to
report the ² _____, a police officer came to
the apartment and looked around. She said that the
³ _____ had probably climbed over the
roofs of the houses behind to ⁴ _____ the
apartment through a window. He had then broken
the lock on the front door to leave. The thief didn't
⁵ _____ much – just some money and an
old camera of mine – but I was shocked that it had been
so easy for him to get into my apartment.

b Read the definitions and complete the missing letters in the crime.

1 entering a building illegally and stealing things from it
   b u r g l a r y

2 killing somebody deliberately
   m _ _ d _ _ _

3 giving money or valuable items to a person to persuade them to help you
   br _ b _ _ _ _

4 following and watching somebody over a long period of time in a way that is annoying or frightening
   st _ _ k _ _ _ _

5 destroying or damaging something, especially public property, deliberately and for no good reason
   v _ _ d _ l _ _ _ _

6 demanding money from a person by threatening to tell somebody else a secret about them
   bl _ _ _ m _ _ _ _

7 using violence or threats to take control of a vehicle, often in order to demand something from a government
   h _ j _ ck _ _ _ _

8 copying money, documents, etc., in order to cheat people
   f _ _ g _ _ _ _

9 using violent action in order to achieve political aims or force a government to act
   t _ _ rr _ _ r _ _ _ _

10 finding a way to look at or change information on somebody else's computer system without permission
   h _ _ ck _ _ _ _

11 stealing something from a person or place
   th _ _ _ _

12 cheating somebody to get money or goods illegally
   fr _ _ _ _

13 stealing money from a bank, store, person, etc., especially using violence or threats
   r _ bb _ _ _ _

14 attacking somebody violently in order to steal their money, especially in a public place
   m _ gg _ _ _ _

15 taking, sending, or bringing goods secretly or illegally into or out of a country
   sm _ _ _ l _ _ _ _

16 taking somebody away illegally and keeping them as a prisoner, especially in order to get money
   k _ _ n _ pp _ _ _ _

c Complete the chart.

criminal	verb
¹ burglar	burglarize
2	murder
✗	bribe
3	stalk
4	vandalize
5	blackmail
6	hijack
7	forge
8	set off bombs, etc.
9	hack
10	steal
11	commit fraud
12	rob
13	mug
14	smuggle
15	kidnap

d Complete the sentences with the past simple form of a verb from **c**.

1 Fortunately, the gang _robbed_ the bank when there were no customers inside.
2 The woman _____ the actor for many years, following him wherever he went.
3 They _____ $1 million worth of electronic goods into the country before they were caught at customs.
4 The construction company _____ the mayor with tens of thousands of dollars for permission to build houses on the land.
5 Two men _____ my friend at knifepoint yesterday. They took all her money.
6 The woman _____ fraud by pretending she was a psychic and charging people.
7 Some teenagers _____ my house while I was away and took all my music equipment.
8 Apparently, she _____ her husband by poisoning him because she was planning to cash in the insurance money.
9 Someone _____ my car from outside my house last night.
10 They _____ the businessman by threatening to send the photographs to his wife if he didn't pay them the money.
11 Two armed men _____ the plane and forced the pilot to take them to the nearest airport.
12 The woman was arrested because she _____ several documents including passports, driver's licenses, and stock certificates.
13 The terrorists _____ a bomb inside a crowded shopping mall.
14 A couple _____ the politician as he left his house and later demanded $1 million for his safe return.
15 Youths _____ the park last night and damaged a lot of trees and flowers.
16 Someone _____ my computer last month and stole my personal details.

e Complete the text with the words in the lists.

Nouns

court   evidence   judge   jury   proof   punishment   verdict   witnesses

Verbs

accused   acquitted   arrest   catch   charged   committed   ~~investigate~~   question   sentenced

It is the job of the police to [1] _investigate_ crimes and try to [2]_____ the criminal or criminals who [3]_____ the crime. When the police have a suspect, they can [4]_____ him or her and take them to the police station to [5]_____ them. If the suspect is [6]_____ with the crime, they have to appear in front of a [7]_____ and maybe a [8]_____ (of 12 people) in [9]_____. Here they are [10]_____ of the crime and [11]_____ may be called to give [12]_____. If there is no [13]_____ that they were involved in the crime, they are [14]_____. If not, they have to wait for the [15]_____. If they are found guilty, they are given a [16]_____. In some cases, they may be [17]_____ to spend a period of time in prison.

2 VOCABULARY FROM READING

Complete the sentences with a word from the list.

~~con~~   claim   hand over   impression   prey   scam   target   wary

1 Be careful when buying something from an unfamiliar website, because someone might try to _con_ you.
2 Fake gas inspectors _____ on elderly people living alone.
3 We were under the _____ that we had rented an apartment, but in fact it didn't exist.
4 The robbers ordered the bank staff to _____ the money if they didn't want to get hurt.
5 He tried to _____ he had made a mistake, but it was obvious he was lying.
6 I'm _____ of giving someone my email address if I don't know them very well.
7 A common _____ in big cities is for a tourist to be sprayed with a liquid and then have their wallet stolen by a person helping to clean the mess.
8 The gang chose to _____ small jewelry stores in the hope that they would be easier to rob.

🔊 Go online for more practice

3 PRONUNCIATION the letter u

a Circle the word with a different sound.

1	**ɜr** bird	**bur**glar **mur**derer **ver**dict (**ve**ry)
2	**ʌ** up	s**u**rroundings dr**u**gs j**u**dge sm**u**ggle
3	**ʊr** tourist	d**u**ring f**u**ture j**u**ry sec**u**re
4	/yu/	acc**u**se comm**u**nity p**u**nish **u**seful
5	**ɔ** saw	c**au**ght g**ui**lty st**a**lker fr**au**d

b 🔊 8.1 Listen and check. Then listen again and repeat the words.

4 GRAMMAR the passive (all forms); *have something done*; *it is said that..., he is thought to...*, etc.

a Complete the text with the correct active or passive form of the verbs in parentheses.

Last month my motorcycle [1] *was taken* (take) from outside my house. When I called the police, I [2] *found out* (find out) that over 20 motorcycles [3] _____ (steal) in my area in the previous six months. The officer I spoke to promised me that the thief would [4] _____ (catch) and punished as soon as possible.

First, the police [5] _____ (question) all the victims of the thefts and [6] _____ (visit) all the motorcycle dealers in the area. Their investigations came to an end late last night when they identified the criminal...as my next-door neighbor!

He [7] _____ (just arrest), and right now he [8] _____ (hold) at the local police station. His case [9] _____ (hear) in court next week and everyone [10] _____ (expect) him to be found guilty. He might [11] _____ (give) a short prison sentence, but the best thing is that no more motorcycles [12] _____ (steal) in my area in the future.

b Rewrite the sentences with *have something done*.

1 Someone is going to change the lock on my front door.
   I'm going to *have the lock on my front door changed*.

2 Someone tests our burglar alarm twice a year.
   We _____ twice a year.

3 A mechanic has repaired my car.
   I _____.

4 Someone broke our windows when we were on vacation.
   We _____ when we were on vacation.

5 Someone will clean my carpets in the spring.
   I _____ in the spring.

6 Someone has hacked my boyfriend's computer.
   My boyfriend _____.

7 Someone cleans Ahmed's apartment once a week.
   Ahmed _____ once a week.

8 A company is redesigning our back yard.
   We _____.

c Complete the second sentence so that it means the same as the first sentence.

1 It is known that the forger is a local man.
   The forger *is known to be a local man*.

2 The blackmailer is understood to be a colleague of the victim.
   It is *understood that the blackmailer is a colleague of the victim*.

3 It is expected that the man will be acquitted.
   The man _____.

4 It is reported that kidnappers have taken the president's wife.
   Kidnappers _____.

5 The terrorists are thought to be in hiding somewhere in France.
   It is _____.

6 The suspect is known to be dangerous.
   It is _____.

7 The police are said to have arrested three men.
   It is _____.

8 It is reported that vandals have damaged several buildings in the area.
   Vandals _____.

d Write an anecdote about a crime that you or someone you know was affected by. Use the passive and causative *have*.

🔴 Go online for more practice

8B Fake news

A newspaper is a device unable to discriminate between a bicycle accident and the collapse of civilization.
George Bernard Shaw, Irish author and playwright

G reporting verbs **V** the media **P** word stress

1 GRAMMAR reporting verbs

a Circle the correct form.

1 I agreed *to meet* / *meeting* my friend next to the information kiosk at Grand Central Terminal.
2 My husband denied *to eat* / *eating* the last piece of cake.
3 Jane promised *to return* / *returning* my book the next day.
4 The tour guide recommended *to visit* / *visiting* the Picasso Museum.
5 The girl refused *to dance* / *dancing* with my friend.
6 The police accused him *to commit* / *of committing* fraud.
7 My boyfriend asked me *to take* / *taking* him to the airport.
8 The teacher threatened *to give* / *giving* them extra homework if they didn't stop talking.
9 Nina's parents told her *not to be* / *not being* late.
10 The woman admitted *to steal* / *stealing* the man's watch.

b Complete the sentences reporting the direct speech using a reporting verb from the list.

~~advise~~   apologize   insist   invite   offer   remind   suggest   warn

1 "I really don't think you should leave your job," Jack's friend told him.
   Jack's friend *advised him not to leave* his job.
2 "I'm going with you to the doctor's, whether you like it or not," Alice said to me.
   Alice _____ to the doctor's with me, whether I liked it or not.
3 "Why don't we go for a walk?" said Katie.
   Katie _____ for a walk.
4 "I'll make lunch," her husband said.
   Her husband _____ lunch.
5 "Don't park there," the man said to us. "You'll get a ticket."
   The man _____ there or we'd get a ticket.
6 "I'm sorry I was so rude," I said.
   I _____ so rude.
7 "Would you like to have dinner with me?" Andy asked Sarah.
   Andy _____ with him.
8 "Don't forget to sign the documents," my boss told me.
   My boss _____ the documents.

c Write about six things that people have said to you today. Use the reporting verbs from **a** and **b**.

1 _____
2 _____
3 _____
4 _____
5 _____
6 _____

2 PRONUNCIATION word stress

a Underline the stressed syllable in the reporting verbs in the list. Then put them in the correct column.

a|ccuse ad|mit ad|vise a|gree con|vince de|ny
in|sist in|vite o|ffer or|der per|suade pro|mise
re|fuse re|gret re|mind sug|gest threa|ten

Stress on first syllable	Stress on second syllable
	accuse

b 🔊 8.2 Listen and check. Then listen and repeat the reporting verbs.

c 🔊 8.3 Listen and complete the sentences.

1 She _offered to_ make lunch.
2 He _____ clean his room.
3 They _____ call the police.
4 She _____ come home early.
5 They _____ give me more time.
6 He _____ her for his behavior.

d 🔊 8.3 Listen again and repeat the sentences. Try to link the verbs and *to* where appropriate.

3 VOCABULARY the media

a Complete the headlines with a verb from the list that means the same as the verb in parentheses.

~~axed~~ back bids clash hit quit
quiz spat split tabbed vows wed

1 **TV series _axed_ after drop in audience figures (cut)**

2 **Singer to _____ Brazilian model (marry)**

3 **Senator to _____ after revelations about personal life (resign)**

4 Police _____ wife after man disappears (question)

5 Hollywood stars _____ presidential candidate (support)

6 **US stock market _____ by new company scandal (badly affected)**

7 **Ex-basketball player _____ to win reality show (predicted)**

8 **Government _____ to invest more money in rural areas (promises)**

9 **TV host fired by ABC in _____ over dress code (argument)**

10 Celebrity couple _____ after five years (separate)

11 **Former lawyer _____ to become country's new president (attempts)**

12 Players _____ over referee's decision (disagree)

Go online for more practice

b Complete the sentences with a media job from the list.

advice columnist   critics   editor
freelance journalist   host   newscaster
~~paparazzi~~   reporter   sports commentator

1 The *paparazzi* were waiting outside the restaurant to photograph the movie star.
2 Have you ever written an email to an _____, asking for advice?
3 I'm surprised none of the _____ liked the movie; I thought it was great!
4 The sports _____ got very excited when the first goal was scored.
5 A _____ at the scene of the crime gave more details about the murder.
6 The newspaper _____ decided not to print the reporter's story because it was too politically sensitive.
7 I stopped watching that show because I can't stand the _____.
8 Laura writes articles for different newspapers as a _____.
9 The _____ was very embarrassed when he couldn't pronounce the politician's name.

c Complete the sentences.

1 The newspaper my father reads is bi*ased* towards the government.
2 It's impossible for a journalist to be ob_____ about a subject on which he or she holds a strong opinion.
3 The article was cen_____ so as not to give away any military secrets.
4 Online papers use sen_____ headlines to make people click on an article and read it.
5 The reporter gave an acc_____ description of events; that's exactly how I remember them.

4 VOCABULARY FROM READING

Complete the chart with the words in the list according to their meaning.

~~doctored~~   exaggerated   fake   false
improbable   legitimate   misleading
reliable   reputable   untrustworthy

can be trusted	can't be trusted

made more dramatic	not true
	doctored

🔵 **Go online** for more practice   ✅ **Go online** to check your progress

> There is only one boss. The customer. And he can fire everybody in the company from the chairman on down, simply by spending his money elsewhere.
> *Sam Walton, founder of Walmart*

G clauses of contrast and purpose | **V** advertising, business | **P** changing stress on nouns and verbs

1 GRAMMAR clauses of contrast and purpose

a Circle the correct word.

1 The restaurant staff members seem happy *despite* / *although* the fact that they work long hours every day.
2 The account manager called his client *for* / *to* arrange a meeting.
3 The company is expanding *even though* / *in spite of* there is a recession.
4 The firm closed several of its smaller office buildings *in order to* / *so that* cut costs.
5 *Although* / *Despite* she's the head of the department, she often goes out with her colleagues after work.
6 I stayed at my desk *to not* / *so as not to* miss an important phone call.
7 Everybody seemed to enjoy Mike's speech at the wedding, *in spite of* / *even though* his terrible jokes.
8 She closed the door of her office *so as to* / *so that* nobody could hear her conversation.
9 I still buy that chocolate bar, *in spite of* / *though* it's much smaller than it used to be.
10 Yuri has to learn English *to* / *for* his job.

b Complete the second sentence so that it has a similar meaning to the first sentence. Use the **bold** word or phrase.

1 Is that a machine to make juice?
   for
   Is that a machine *for making juice* _____?
2 The store closed down even though it was in an ideal location.
   in spite of
   The store closed down _____.
3 They reduced their prices so as to sell more products.
   so that
   They reduced their prices _____.
4 I have to leave work by six o'clock so that I don't miss my train.
   in order not to
   I have to leave work by six o'clock _____.
5 Despite the fact that I was very late, my boss wasn't angry.
   although
   My boss wasn't angry _____.
6 Although she's the managing director, she doesn't have her own office
   despite
   She doesn't have her own office _____.

2 VOCABULARY advertising, business

a Complete the sentences with a word from the list.

advertisement̶ advertising campaign
be sued brand claim consumer
misleading publicity slogan

1 There are lots of websites where you can put an
  _advertisement_____ if you want to sell your car.
2 As a _____, I want to have as much
  information about the food I buy as possible.
3 I always buy the same _____ of
  toothpaste because it's the one I'm used to.
4 They've used young adults in their new
  _____ because it's aimed specifically
  at people in their early 20s.
5 It's _____ to suggest that this product
  is healthier than any others of its kind – it isn't.
6 Their company _____ only has three
  words: *Just do it.*
7 There has been a lot of _____ about
  the company owner's recent charity donation.
8 A company can _____ if it doesn't
  fulfill the promises it makes about its products.
9 A representative denied the _____
  that the company was in financial difficulties.

b Read the definitions and complete the missing
letters in the word.

1 the main office of a company
  h e a d o f f i c e
2 a group of stores or hotels owned by the same
  company
  ch __ __ n
3 stop trading or doing business
  cl __ __ __ d __ w __
4 an office or a store belonging to a large company or
  organization
  br __ n __ __
5 a difficult time for the economy of a country
  r __ c __ __ __ i __ __
6 a period of sudden economic growth
  b __ o __
7 a product that is not successful
  fl __ __
8 fall; become lower or less
  d __ o __
9 make goods in large quantities, using machinery
  m __ n __ __ __ __ t __ __ __
10 combine to form a single thing
  m __ __ g __

c Complete the text with the correct form of the
verbs and verb phrases in the list.

become the market leader expand export grow
import launch a new product market produce
set up a new business̶ take over

A friend of mine, Anne, was lucky
enough to inherit a farm when she
graduated from college, so she decided
to [1] _set up a new business_: an organic
food company. The company
[2] _____ its products
under the name Bioplus, and among
other things, it [3] _____ granola. Anne
[4] _____ nuts and dried fruit from South
America and mixes these with cereal from crops on the
farm to make the granola. Her granola sells well regionally,
and recently she [5] _____ into new markets
on the East Coast. Today, she also [6] _____ to
neighboring countries, like Canada and Mexico.
  The company is [7] _____ rapidly, and Anne is
always looking for new employees. Right now, she's preparing
to [8] _____: a cereal bar the company has been
testing. Anne is very realistic because she knows she will
never [9] _____ in the field. However, neither
does she want one of the big cereal giants, like Kelloggs or
Nestlé, to [10] _____ her small family company.

d Complete the sentences with the correct form of
make or *do*.

1 A company always _does_____ extensive market
  research before it launches a new product.
2 If a company _____ a loss, the staff members
  often face job cuts.
3 Many countries started _____ business with
  China when the trade sanctions were lifted.
4 The managing director _____ the decision to
  close the factory yesterday.
5 The factory owner may lose his business because he
  _____ several risky investments.
6 My company _____ really badly last year; if the
  situation doesn't improve, it may close.
7 Management and unions have _____ a deal that
  should prevent a strike.
8 If we _____ a profit again next year, the manager
  may think of opening another office.
9 There's no need to thank me. I'm only _____ my
  job.
10 She doesn't _____ much money from acting, so
  she also has a part-time job as a server.

🔄 **Go online** for more practice

e Match 1–8 to responses a–h.

1 Where have you been? __c__
2 Let's start the meeting. ____
3 I'm going out with my boss for dinner tonight. ____
4 Let's go to that trendy café on the corner. ____
5 Let's finish the meeting. ____
6 Who are you texting? ____
7 Your boss is heading in this direction. ____
8 Why do you need to talk to your ex? ____

a Yes, let's get down to business.
b I'm afraid it's gone out of business.
c ~~Mind your own business!~~
d Are you sure you want to mix business with pleasure?
e OK, but first, is there any other business?
f I'm sorry, but it's none of your business.
g Because we have some unfinished business.
h Yes, and it looks as if she means business.

f Answer the questions about yourself and your home.

1 How far from your home is the nearest branch of your bank?

_____

2 Name a chain that you can find in your nearest shopping mall.

_____

3 Which products are manufactured in your country?

_____

4 Which companies from your country are market leaders?

_____

5 Which products does your country export and where to?

_____

6 Which industries are growing in your country?

_____

7 Which products does your country import and where from?

_____

8 Would you like to set up your own company? Why / Why not?

_____

3 PRONUNCIATION changing stress on nouns and verbs

a <u>U</u>nderline the stressed syllable in the highlighted words.

1 China exports more goods than any other country.
2 They transport most of their products by truck.
3 There's been a huge increase in gas prices recently.
4 The price of wheat has decreased by 5%.
5 Scientists are making progress in finding a cure for AIDS.
6 The visa permits you to stay for three months.
7 Brazil produces about a third of the world's coffee.
8 We do not give refunds without a valid receipt.
9 The government is hoping to reduce foreign imports.
10 Vinyl records are becoming popular again.

b ◖9.1 Listen and check. Then listen again and repeat the sentences.

Go online for more practice

9B Super cities

A city is a large community where people are lonely together.
Herbert Prochnow, US banking executive

| G uncountable and plural nouns | V word building: prefixes and suffixes | P word stress with prefixes and suffixes |

1 GRAMMAR uncountable and plural nouns

a Circle the correct answers. Check (✓) if both answers are possible.

1 Can I have *a piece of bread / some bread*, please? ✓
2 My grandmother suffers from *bad health / a bad health*.
3 I bought *a new piece of furniture / some new furniture* for my living room.
4 Can you please give me *a piece of advice / some advice*?
5 We lost *a luggage / a piece of luggage* on the way back from Singapore.
6 Jackie's upset because she got *a bad news / some bad news*.
7 Be careful with that vase – it's made of *glass / a glass*.
8 My girlfriend gave me *a pair of pajamas / some pajamas* for my birthday.
9 The teacher gave the boy extra points for *a good behavior / good behavior*.
10 Can you lend me *a paper / some paper*? I left my notebook at home.

b Complete the sentences with *is* or *are*.

1 My clothes _are_ really wet. I got caught in a thunderstorm.
2 Police _____ investigating the murder of an elderly woman in her home.
3 The hotel staff members _____ always really polite and helpful.
4 The new research into sleep patterns _____ fascinating.
5 The outskirts of the town _____ run-down and a little bit depressing.
6 The good news _____ that we're getting married in the spring!
7 The flight crew on this plane _____ very young.
8 Politics _____ really fascinating – particularly for politicians!
9 Do you think my belongings _____ safe in the hotel room?
10 The traffic _____ terrible in the rush hour in the city.

c Complete the sentences with information that is true for you.

1 The scenery in this area _____
_____
_____.

2 The traffic in my area _____
_____
_____.

3 My clothes _____
_____
_____.

4 The furniture in my home _____
_____
_____.

5 The news today _____
_____
_____.

6 Politics in my country _____
_____
_____.

7 The weather today _____
_____
_____.

8 My family _____
_____
_____.

2 VOCABULARY word building: prefixes and suffixes

a Complete the sentences with a prefix from the list.

anti auto bi mega mis mono
multi over post ~~sub~~ under

1 Some of the residents of megacities live in _sub___standard housing of very poor quality.

2 There was a food shortage in many countries during the _____-war period between 1946 and 1960.

3 Hundreds of fans were waiting for the singer, hoping to get an _____graph.

4 My English teacher recommends us to use a _____lingual dictionary – one that is only in English.

5 My colleagues are always complaining that they are _____worked and _____paid. They say they work long hours and are badly paid.

6 The leader of the protest used a _____phone to make himself heard.

7 You couldn't miss Sandra – she was the one in the _____colored coat. It was green, purple, yellow, and orange, I think.

8 The town has just celebrated its _____centennial – it was founded 200 years ago.

9 The doctor prescribed _____biotics for my brother's chest infection.

10 It's a popular _____conception that cold weather can give you a cold. This is simply not true.

b Complete the sentences. Add -able, -ful, -less, or -proof to a word from the list.

~~break~~ bullet care drink home hope use water

1 Is there anything _breakable___ in this box?

2 Be _____ crossing that road – there's always a lot of traffic.

3 Don't forget to take a _____ jacket with you when you go hiking in the mountains.

4 This _____ gadget opens jars for people who have no strength in their hands.

5 Alexi became _____ when he was downsized and could no longer pay his rent.

6 The police officer wasn't injured because he was wearing a _____ vest.

7 Is the tap water _____ in this area?

8 It's _____ asking the boss for a pay raise – the company is losing money.

c Complete the sentences with the noun form of the word in parentheses.

1 I borrowed the money with the _intention___ of giving it back to you. (intend)

2 His greatest _____ is his inability to express his feelings. (weak)

3 I was away for six months, and there were many changes in my _____. (absent)

4 If you witness an act of _____, you are advised to call the police. (vandal)

5 _____ is one of the greatest problems the elderly have to face. (lonely)

6 Teachers are trying to fight _____ in schools throughout the country. (race)

7 Most of her problems are the result of a very unhappy _____. (child)

8 The best thing about our hotel was that it provided _____ in the evenings. (entertain)

9 There's been a great _____ in public transportation recently. (improve)

10 The _____ of online shopping means that fewer people are shopping in the malls. (convenient)

11 What's the _____ between Montreal and Toronto? (distant)

12 Gandhi was a humanist who believed in the _____ of man. (brother)

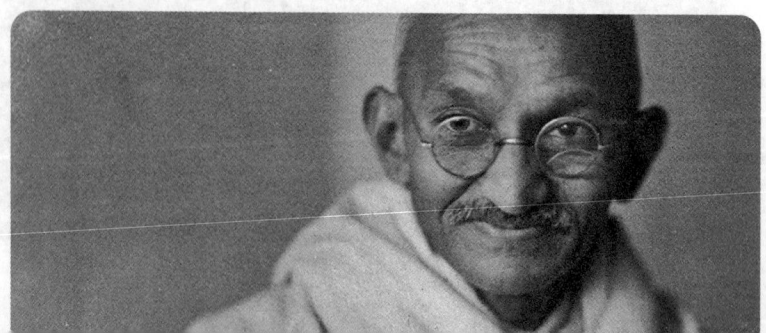

⟳ **Go online** for more practice

d Complete the second sentence with the noun form of the **bold** word in the first sentence.

1 I **believe** that house prices are going to rise.
It's my _belief_ that house prices are going to rise.

2 The staff members were shocked when their boss **died**.
The staff members were shocked at the _____ of their boss.

3 You shouldn't go out when it's **hot** during the day.
You shouldn't go out during the _____ of the day.

4 You need to measure how **wide** the windows are.
You need to measure the _____ of your windows.

5 I can't believe you're still **hungry** after that huge meal.
I can't believe that huge meal didn't satisfy your _____.

6 The company may **lose** financially on this deal.
The company might take a financial _____ on this deal.

7 Do you know how **high** Mount Everest is?
Do you know the _____ of Mount Everest?

8 I don't like to **think** of you walking home alone.
I don't like the _____ of you walking home alone.

9 After his illness, they gave him soup to make him **strong** again.
After his illness, they gave him soup to build up his _____ again.

10 The dinner party was very **successful**.
The dinner party was a great _____.

3 VOCABULARY FROM READING

Complete the sentences with a word or phrase from the list.

---
a lack of   delivers   echoes   head home   perks
~~sparsely populated~~   sprawling   state-of-the-art

1 Mongolia is one of the most _sparsely populated_ countries in the world – there are only five people per square mile.

2 I have a long commute, so I always _____ right after work.

3 One of the _____ of city life is the numerous entertainment options.

4 In many big cities there's _____ green spaces to walk or just sit and relax.

5 The design of the museum _____ that of a palace.

6 Our new home _____ on comfort but looks out on an industrial estate.

7 Los Angeles is recognized as the most _____ city in the US because it covers such a large area of land.

8 The company has just launched a new line of _____ computers.

4 PRONUNCIATION word stress with prefixes and suffixes

a Underline the main stressed syllable in the words in the list. Then put them in the correct column.

~~an|ti|so|cial~~   bi|ling|ual   con|ven|ience   en|ter|tain|ment
ex|cite|ment   friend|li|ness   go|vern|ment   ig|no|rance
o|ver|crow|ded   po|ver|ty   re|duc|tion   un|em|ploy|ment

Stress on first syllable	Stress on second syllable	Stress on third syllable
		antisocial

b ◑9.2 Listen and check. Then listen and repeat the words.

◔ **Go online** for more practice   ◉ **Go online** to check your progress

8 & 9 Colloquial English Advertising

1 LOOKING AT LANGUAGE

Complete the sentences with a phrase from the list.

~~an ear worm~~   a captive audience   get into your head
had their day   hit a false note   their ears perk up
word for word

1 The best way to get rid of <u>an ear worm</u> is to replace it with another tune.
2 Some people say that libraries have _____ and they will soon disappear.
3 The song has a catchy chorus that can easily _____ and you find yourself singing it all day.
4 I repeated her instructions _____ to avoid any confusion.
5 My dogs love dog biscuits – _____ as soon as they hear me open the package.
6 Musicians often play in train stations and ask for money because they know they have _____.
7 The politician _____ with her speech and caused a lot of controversy.

2 VOCABULARY FROM THE INTERVIEW

Complete the sentences from the interview with a word from the list.

~~baton~~   bet   fan   gold   short   tapped

1 I took the <u>baton</u> from him.
2 I _____ you most people would remember these commercials.
3 Using a celebrity is a _____ cut.
4 I'm not a big _____ of it.
5 They _____ into a mindset.
6 They became the _____ standard.

3 THE CONVERSATION

Match beginnings 1–6 to endings a–f.

1 Just by going outside you're seeing these advertisements and you're being influenced, so, for example we, <u>d</u>
2 You know, we barely, ____
3 So, there's definitely, ____
4 They see pictures in magazines and they're starting to be, ____
5 Yeah, especially for children, I mean I, I have, ____
6 So, I think, um, I think, ____

a we don't really watch TV and we have a TV; we just don't watch very much.
b definitely I think that the answer to the question is yes, we are all influenced in different ways by advertising, I suppose.
c I have younger siblings and it's kind of like "Oh, all of my friends have this toy; I must have it as well"…
d ~~we all know certain brands just because they're everywhere around us.~~
e you're definitely being influenced.
f my 11-year-old is starting to be a little bit more cynical about what he sees.

4 VOCABULARY FROM THE CONVERSATION

~~blatant~~   point   subtle   rush   subliminally

1 So that sort of advertising is <u>blatant</u>.
2 And that's super-_____ advertising.
3 You might buy this if you're in a _____.
4 _____, I think, if we recognize something…
5 The _____ of advertisements is that you recognize the products.

GRAMMAR & VOCABULARY

a Complete the second sentence so that it means the same as the first sentence. Write 2–5 words. Use the word in parentheses.

1 Owen started studying at 9:00 a.m. and he's still studying now, at 6:00 p.m. (has)
Owen _____ all day.

2 We aren't very excited about climbing, so we didn't go to the mountains. (much)
We didn't go to the mountains because we don't like _____.

3 I don't have Shen's number, so I can't call him. (his)
I'd call Shen if I _____.

4 Inez still finds it strange to live on her own. She really doesn't like it. (get)
Inez can't _____ on her own. She really doesn't like it.

5 I can't wait to see you next week. (looking)
I'm _____ next week.

6 I'll always remember the first time I visited Florence. I fell in love with the city. (forget)
I'll _____ for the first time. I fell in love with the city.

7 I'm sure you left your jacket in the car. You weren't wearing it when you came in. (have)
You _____ in the car. You weren't wearing it when you came in.

8 I get the impression that Emily has been crying. (as)
It _____ has been crying.

9 We asked a plumber to fix our shower. (had)
We _____ by a plumber.

10 His teacher said he should enter the writing competition. (encouraged)
His teacher _____ the writing competition.

11 I arrived on time, although I had left home late. (despite)
_____, I arrived on time

12 Laura bought some new shorts that were on sale. (a)
Laura bought _____ that were on sale.

b Complete the text. Write one word in each blanks.

India set to break world records

It would seem that Tokyo is about to lose its position [1]_____ the largest city in the world. According to the UN, Delhi, the capital of India, is set to take the top spot in 2028. The organization predicts that Delhi's population will [2]_____ grown from 29 million to 39 million [3]_____ 2030. Meanwhile, it [4]_____ thought that Tokyo's population will remain at its current level of 37 million.

In [5]_____, it is not only India's capital city that is likely to break records soon, but the country itself. The population of India is expected [6]_____ reach 1.438 billion in 2024, exceeding China's 1.436 billion. This increase would make India the most populous country in the world.

Delhi is not the only city in India where significant population growth is predicted to [7]_____ place. The population of Mumbai is set to rise from 19 million to 25 million. In [8]_____ of this growth, the city will maintain its position as the world's sixth-largest city. [9]_____ though the population of Kolkata will increase from 14 million to 18 million, the city will move down the list, from 13th to 16th position. Bengaluru, which is ranked 29th [10]_____ this time, will move up to the 21st spot as its population grows from 10 million to 16 million.

10A Science fact, science fiction

> In science the credit goes to the man who convinces the world, not to the man to whom the idea first occurs.
> *Francis Darwin, botanist and son of Charles Darwin*

G quantifiers: *all, every, both,* etc. **V** science **P** stress in word families

1 VOCABULARY & PRONUNCIATION
science; stress in word families

a Circle a, b, or c.

1 He's working as a biology teacher although he's a qualified ____.
   a zoology b zoologist c zoological
2 There are thousands of human ____ diseases.
   a genetics b geneticist c genetic
3 My partner has a degree in ____.
   a physics b physicist c physical
4 The results of ____ research have increased the range of medicines available to treat many illnesses.
   a botany b botanist c botanical
5 I'm the only ____ in my family.
   a science b scientist c scientific
6 I wasn't very good at ____ when I was in school.
   a chemistry b chemist c chemical
7 It is thought that there is a ____ reason for his aggressive behavior.
   a biology b biologist c biological
8 My sister is fascinated by space; she's hoping to become an ____.
   a astronomy b astronomer c astronomical

b Underline the stressed syllable in the words. Is the stress on the same syllable? Check (✓) the correct column.

	same syllable	different syllable
1 a|<u>stro</u>|no|my / a|<u>stro</u>|no|mer	✓	
2 bi|o|lo|gy / bi|o|lo|gi|cal		
3 bo|ta|ny / bo|ta|ni|cal		
4 che|mist / che|mi|stry		
5 ge|ne|tic / ge|ne|ti|cist		
6 phy|sics / phy|si|cist		
7 sci|en|tist / sci|en|ti|fic		
8 zo|o|lo|gist / zo|o|lo|gi|cal		

c 10.1 Listen and check. Then listen again and repeat the words.

d Complete the text with the nouns and verbs in the lists.

Verbs

carry out clone ~~do~~ prove volunteer

Nouns

clinical trials discovery drugs guinea pigs ~~pharmaceutical companies~~

Thousands of scientists are employed in [1] *pharmaceutical companies* to [2] *do* ____ research into new [3] ____. These people hope to make an important [4] ____ that will help treat or cure an illness or disease. When a team believes they have developed a new drug, they have to [5] ____ experiments to [6] ____ their theory and make sure the drug is effective. The final stage of this process is to organize [7] ____ so that the drug can be tested on humans. People who [8] ____ to take part in these tests are known as [9] ____, after the animals that were used in 19th-century medical research. If the tests are successful, the drug is launched onto the market.

One branch of science that is becoming increasingly important in these companies is genetics. Genetic engineers have already managed to [10] ____ a number of different animals, including sheep, rabbits, and monkeys.

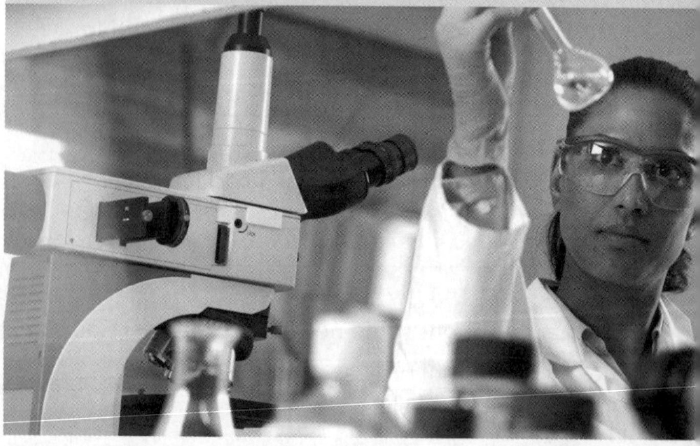

2 VOCABULARY FROM LISTENING

Match the words in the list to the definitions.

dissolve ~~gas~~ gravity moist particle
reflect rotate scatter water vapor

1 any substance like air that is neither a solid nor a liquid
_gas_____

2 mix with a liquid and become part of it _____

3 a very small piece of something _____

4 make things move very quickly in different directions
_____

5 water in the form of a gas resulting from heating water or ice _____

6 show the image of somebody / something on the surface of, e.g., a mirror _____

7 slightly wet _____

8 move or turn around a central fixed point _____

9 the force that causes objects to fall to the ground when they are dropped _____

3 VOCABULARY FROM READING

Complete the highlighted words and phrases that express degrees of likelihood.

1 The new measures could, in th _e_ _o_ r _y_, reduce pollution in the city dramatically.

2 It seems pl _ _ _ s _ b _ _ _ _ that sea levels may rise dramatically in the near future.

3 The idea that we'll ever colonize space seems rather f _ _ _ _ -f _ tch _ _ _ to me.

4 We're still a l _ _ _ g way from finding a source of energy to replace fossil fuels completely.

5 Slowing global warming might be ach _ _ _ v _ b _ _ _ if every country cooperates.

6 The time when I will be able to afford to stop working is quite a w _ _ _ off.

7 The poorest countries still face extreme obst _ c _ _ s to development; for example, corruption.

8 The idea that one day cars will fly is not totally impl _ _ _ s _ b _ _ _.

9 It might be p _ ss _ b _ _ _ to see Mars in the sky tonight, if conditions are right.

10 There is a r _ _ _ l possibility that it might snow tomorrow.

11 The theory is only sp _ c _ l _ t _ v _ right now. Much more evidence is needed before it can be proved for certain.

4 GRAMMAR quantifiers: all, every, both, etc.

a Right (✓) or wrong (✗)? Correct the mistakes in the highlighted phrases.

1 I've taken all luggage up to our room, OK?
   ✗ _all the luggage_

2 Everybody were bad-tempered because it was getting late and they were hungry.
   _____

3 All went wrong at my last job interview.
   _____

4 I have a lot of cousins, but most of them live abroad. _____

5 Every classroom in that school has an interactive whiteboard. _____

6 My mom works as a volunteer at the hospital every morning. _____

7 The most people are against eating genetically modified food. _____

8 All the men seem to love buying new electronic gadgets. _____

⊙ Go online for more practice

b Complete the conversations with *no, any,* or *none.*

1 **A** Can I have a cookie?
 B Sorry, we don't have *any*_____.

2 **A** How much homework have you done?
 B _____. I don't feel like doing it right now.

3 **A** How are we going to get home?
 B By taxi. There aren't _____ buses at this time of night.

4 **A** Did any of your friends pass the exam?
 B No, _____ of them. It was too difficult.

5 **A** Let's have dinner in our hotel room.
 B We can't. There's _____ room service after 9 p.m.

6 **A** When can you come?
 B _____ day you like. I'm free all week.

c Complete the sentences with a word from the list. Use each word twice.

both   either   neither   nor

1 *Both*_____ my brother and my sister have children.

2 Dave has two sons, but _____ of them looks like him.

3 We'd like to go to _____ Sayulita or Cabo San Lucas for our vacation this year.

4 Neither my boyfriend _____ I eat meat.

5 I can't decide between these two shirts. I like _____ of them.

6 _____ of my parents have ever been to South America.

7 My niece is studying _____ chemistry or biology in college – I can't remember which.

8 Her son neither calls _____ messages me when he's away.

d Complete the text. Write one word in each blank.

Irène and Ève Curie:
the scientist and the journalist

Nearly [1]*everyone*_____ knows the names of scientists Marie and Pierre Curie because of the Nobel Prizes they won. However, [2]_____ people are unaware that the couple also had two talented daughters, Irène and Ève. [3]_____ sisters received the same education, but they each pursued a completely different career.

Irène followed in the footsteps of her parents. She began assisting her mother during World War I, when she was only 18. The two women used some of the first X-ray machines to help doctors locate the exact position of soldiers' injuries. At the time, people had [4]_____ idea of the dangers posed by the machines, and nurses who used them didn't wear [5]_____ protection. As a result, Irène and her mother were exposed to large doses of radiation and [6]_____ of them lived to a very old age.

In 1924, Irène was asked to share her research techniques with a chemical engineer named Frédéric Joliot. They started going out together, but Marie was afraid that Joliot was only interested in becoming associated with the Curie name. She used [7]_____ her influence to try to end the relationship, but Irène took [8]_____ of her advice, and the couple later married. Irène and her husband continued working together, and in 1935 they too were awarded a Nobel Prize.

Ève Curie, on the other hand, preferred the arts and spent most of her time [9]_____ writing or playing the piano. She worked as a journalist and wrote her mother's biography *Madame Curie*, which was published in 1937. Her husband, Henry Richardson Labouisse, was Executive Director of UNICEF, and when the organization was awarded the Nobel Peace Prize in 1965, he collected the award. Ève used to joke that [10]_____ member of her family had received a Nobel Prize except for her.

Irène Joliot-Curie died in Paris in 1956 at the age of 58. Ève Curie was 102 when she passed away in New York in 2007.

Go online for more practice

There are always three speeches for every one you actually gave: the one you practiced, the one you gave, and the one you wish you had given.
Dale Carnegie, American lecturer

G articles | **V** collocation: word pairs | **P** pausing and sentence stress

1 GRAMMAR articles

a Complete the sayings with *a*, *an*, *the*, or no article (–).

1 All you need is __–__ love.
2 He's _____ man of his word.
3 _____ women are from Venus; _____ men are from Mars.
4 _____ time waits for no man.
5 Don't worry! It isn't _____ end of _____ world!
6 That's _____ life!
7 It's _____ small world!
8 _____ actions speak louder than _____ words.

b Complete the sentences with *the* where necessary.

1 __–__ Mount Aconcagua is in *the* Andes in Argentina.
2 There are 50 states in _____ US.
3 _____ 5 Freeway was closed yesterday because of floods.
4 _____ Central Park is one of _____ largest green spaces in New York City.
5 _____ US Virgin Islands are a group of islands situated in _____ Caribbean Sea.
6 _____ Lake Victoria is the largest lake in _____ Africa.
7 _____ Panama Canal connects the Atlantic Ocean to _____ Pacific Ocean.
8 The toy industry in _____ China is the biggest in the world.

c Right (✓) or wrong (✗)? Correct the mistakes in the highlighted phrases.

1 The church in my village dates back to the 15th century. ✓ _____
2 Mae-Ting can't still be at the work. It's really late. ✗ *at work* _____
3 The college in my town has a very good reputation. _____
4 Daisy is taking advantage of the time her children are at the school to take an online course. _____
5 The prison is on the outskirts of the city. _____
6 Somebody broke into my parents' house while they were at the church. _____
7 Did you have time to finish the work I left for you? _____
8 My boyfriend is in the college. He's studying architecture. _____
9 The man has gone to the prison for the crimes he committed when he was younger. _____
10 My brother teaches at the elementary school he went to when he was a child. _____

d Read the text. Circle a, b, or c.

Five words
that made history

At the 2018 Golden Globe Awards, actress and TV host Oprah Winfrey was awarded the Cecil B. DeMille Award for lifetime achievement. Here is an extract from the memorable speech she made during the award ceremony.

In 1964, I was ¹_____ little girl sitting on the linoleum floor of my mother's house in ²_____ Milwaukee, watching Anne Bancroft present the Oscar for Best Actor at ³_____ 36th Academy Awards. She opened the envelope and said five words that literally made ⁴_____ history: "⁵_____ winner is Sidney Poitier." Up to the stage came ⁶_____ most elegant man I had ever seen. I remember his tie was white and, of course, his skin was black. And I'd never seen ⁷_____ black man being celebrated like that. And I have tried many, many, many times to explain what ⁸_____ moment like that means to a little girl, a kid watching from the cheap seats as my mom came through the door, bone tired from cleaning ⁹_____ other people's houses. But all I can do is quote and say that ¹⁰_____ explanation's in Sidney's performance in *Lilies of the Field*, "Amen, amen. Amen, amen."

1	**a** a	**b** the	**c** –
2	**a** a	**b** the	**c** –
3	**a** a	**b** the	**c** –
4	**a** a	**b** the	**c** –
5	**a** A	**b** The	**c** –
6	**a** a	**b** the	**c** –
7	**a** a	**b** the	**c** –
8	**a** a	**b** the	**c** –
9	**a** a	**b** the	**c** –
10	**a** a	**b** the	**c** –

Go online for more practice

---

2 VOCABULARY collocation: word pairs

a Match questions 1–10 to responses a–j.

1 Did you hear the storm last night? _h_
2 Do you think I should accept the job? _____
3 Why are you moving to the country? _____
4 Why has the store sold out of bread? _____
5 How was your meeting? _____
6 What did you do while you were waiting at the hospital? _____
7 Why does water boil when you heat it? _____
8 What should I do about the argument I had with my sister? _____
9 Why is the playground closed? _____
10 My bike was stolen because I forgot to lock it up. _____

a I'd forgive and forget if I were you.
b Oh well, you live and learn, I guess.
c I paced backwards and forwards in the corridor.
d You need to weigh the pros and cons to help you make a decision.
e It's the law of cause and effect.
f I guess it's a question of supply and demand.
g Short and sweet – it only lasted ten minutes.
h Yes, the thunder and lightning woke me up.
i We're looking for some peace and quiet.
j For health and safety reasons.

b Find the word pairs in the list and link them with *or*. Then complete the sentences.

~~alive~~ all ~~dead~~ later less more never
nothing now once rain right shine
sooner twice wrong

1 The criminal was wanted *dead or alive* and there was a $500 reward for his capture.
2 She goes jogging every morning, _____.
3 I'm not sure if this answer in my math homework is _____.
4 Patricia is about to leave, so it's _____ – I may not get another chance to ask her out.
5 It's _____ with Kim; either she calls every day or you don't hear from her for weeks.
6 I've been skiing _____, but I'm not very good at it.
7 Yiming has _____ finished his homework – all he has to do now is to print it out.
8 There's no point waiting – I'll have to tell John the truth _____.

c Complete the word-pair idioms.

1 We only take a few o*dds* and e*nds* with us when we go on vacation.
2 I'm s_____ and t_____ of having to clean up after my children.
3 B_____ and l_____, I'd say I had a happy childhood.
4 She's fine now, but it was t_____ and g_____ as to whether she would survive the operation.
5 The streets were very dangerous because of the lack of l_____ and o_____ in the city.
6 We arrived s_____ and s_____ after a difficult three-day journey through the mountains.
7 I have no idea what we're having for my birthday lunch because my wife told me to w_____ and s_____.
8 We go to the movies n_____ and a_____, but more often than not, we just watch a movie on TV.

3 VOCABULARY FROM READING

Complete the missing vowels in the words and phrases.

1 A speaker doesn't have to be a comedian to include a little w_it in his or her speech.
2 Salespeople need to have the g __ ft of g __ b to sell as many products as possible.
3 That politician is very good at making memorable s __ __ nd b __ t __ s when he talks to journalists.
4 Barack Obama is famous for being a great __ r __ t __ r who made powerful speeches.

4 PRONUNCIATION pausing and sentence stress

a ◀) 10.2 Listen to a talk about an interesting place to visit. Mark the pauses.

Good morning, and thank you for coming. I'm here to talk about an interesting place to visit in my country. I'm going to tell you about the city of Poughkeepsie in upstate New York. Poughkeepsie is on the Hudson River, and it has one of the world's longest elevated pedestrian walking bridges, measuring 1.28 miles. The city is famous for Locust Grove, the home of Samuel F.B. Morse, the inventor of Morse Code. It has several beautiful colleges, such as Vassar College and Marist College. Poughkeepsie is full of museums, independent stores, and wonderful places to eat and drink. The city is easily accessible from New York City by train, and it is perfect for a day trip or a weekend break.

b Practice giving the talk, pausing and trying to get the right rhythm.

c Now write your own talk about an interesting place to visit in your country. Mark the pauses.

d Read your speech. If you can, record it on your phone and send it to your teacher.

🔾 Go online for more practice   ✅ Go online to check your progress

OXFORD
UNIVERSITY PRESS

198 Madison Avenue
New York, NY 10016 USA

Great Clarendon Street, Oxford, OX2 6DP, United Kingdom

Oxford University Press is a department of the University of Oxford.
It furthers the University's objective of excellence in research, scholarship,
and education by publishing worldwide. Oxford is a registered trade
mark of Oxford University Press in the UK and in certain other countries

ISBN: 978 0 19 490691 3
Printed in China
This book is printed on paper from certified and well-managed sources

ACKNOWLEDGMENTS
*The authors would like to thank all the teachers and students around the world whose feedback
has helped us to shape* American English File.

The authors would also like to thank: all those at Oxford University Press (both in
Oxford and around the world) and the design team who have contributed their
skills and ideas to producing this course.

*Finally very special thanks from Clive to Maria Angeles, Lucia, and Eric, and from Christina
to Cristina, for all their support and encouragement. Christina would also like to thank her
children Joaquin, Marco, and Krysia for their constant inspiration.*

*The authors and publisher are grateful to those who have given permission to reproduce the
following extracts and adaptations of copyright material:* p22 Adapted from *Mini Sagas*
by Brian Aldiss (ed.), *The Daily Telegraph*, © Telegraph Media Group Limited 2013.
Reproduced by permission.

*The publisher would like to thank the following for their permission to reproduce
photographs:* Cover: Hobbit/Shutterstock. Alamy Stock Photo pp6 (interview/
Mariusz Szczawinski), 15 (Tet Festival/ Danita Delimont), 27 (children watching
solar eclipse/Cavan), 35 (bookcase/David Askham), 39 (rescue team/Royal Thai
Navy/UPI), 50 (knee/Fitness People by Vision), 50 (calf/Simon Balson), 53 (rehearsal/
Keith Morris), 57 (Grand Central Station/Steve Tulley), 59 (reporter/Hongqi Zhang),
62 (bank/Clarence Holmes Photography), 63 (traffic/D A Barnes), 64 (Lagos/Ton
Koene), 64 (Mahatma Gandhi/Dinodia Photos), 70 (Marie Curie/Lebrecht Music &
Arts), 72 (Oprah Winfrey/PictureLux/The Hollywood Archive); Getty Images pp7
(driving/Hero Images), 11 (Bermuda Triangle/Lightguard), 17 (friends walking/
Hinterhaus Productions), 22 (empty plate/Blend Images - JGI/Jamie Grill), 26
(sleeping/Peopleimages), 26 (birthday/Caiaimage/Paul Bradbury), 30 (shopping/
urbazon), 40 (tired/Motortion), 43 (playing guitar/Inti St Clair), 44 (cello/Greg Dale),
44 (keyboard/Dave King), 50 (ankle/Jason LaVeris/FilmMagic), 50 (wrist/George
Pimentel/WireImage), 50 (waist/MJ Kim), 50 (fist/JazzIRT), 53 (Juilliard Orchestra/
Hiroyuki Ito) 68 (researcher/Westend61) 73 (walkway/SandyTambone); iStock.com
p50 (hip/John Sommer); OUP pp36 (burrows/Toby Burrows), 44 (soprano/posztos),
44 (bass/Tetra Images), 44 (choir/posztos), 44 (flute/Triff), 44 (violin/Dario Sabljak),
44 (saxophone/horiyan), 44 (drums/misha), 44 (orchestra/Ferenc Szelepcsenyi), 49
(cat/Voraorn Ratanakorn), 63 (Detian Waterfall/4045), 67 (Kolkata/Radiokafka), 71
(Aconcagua/Johnathan Esper), 71 (baby/alice-photo), 71 (teacher/Monkey Business
Images), 72 (storm/Wesley Aston), Science Photo Library pp50 (brain/Sciepro), 50
(kidneys/Sciepro), 50 (liver/Sciepro), 50 (bottom/Ian Hooton), 50 (heart/Sciepro), 50
(lungs/Sciepro); Shutterstock pp4 (tourists/Atstock Productions), 5 (Rio De Janeiro/
SNEHIT), 8 (angry boy/Alexxndr), 9 (Mars/Jurik Peter), 15 (learning sign language/
Andrey_Popov), 16 (house/Christopher Meder), 19 (plane cabin/Vetal), 21 (London/
Javen), 22 (woman/Antonio Guillem), 22 (argument/VGstockstudio), 23 (father &
daughter/Iakov Filimonov), 23 (clothes shopping/Syda Productions), 25 (reading/
Halfpoint), 26 (beach/aveseen), 26 (train journey/Alexey Sizov), 26 (office worker/
Muk Photo), 26 (couple eating/Monkey Business Images), 26 (meeting/Monkey
Business Images), 26 (traveller/AJR_photo), 28 (snowy street/FashionStock.com), 29
(Brooklyn/Brian Goodman), 30 (grandfather & grandson/Rawpixel.com), 32 (Machu
Picchu/lovelypeace), 34 (flight attendant/Sergey Smolentsev), 34 (hiker/David
Varga), 34 (sleep/Monkey Business Images), 35 (sad girl/fizkes), 37 (businessman/
William Perugini), 37 (insomnia/Sergey Mironov), 41 (library/SpeedKingz), 41
(cycling/Brian A Jackson), 41 (sandcastles/oliveromg), 41 (construction worker/
Dmitry Bunin), 42 (business meeting/VGstockstudio), 43 (boy in tree/KaliAntye),
44 (orchestra/Martin Good), 45 (Swan Lake/Jack.Q), 45 (croissant/Yakobchuk
Viacheslav), 46 (missed train/encierro), 47 (bike accident/B-D-S Piotr Marcinski),
47 (plane window/Travel man), 48 (rainy picnic/Robert Wydro Studio), 49 (cake/
Irina Kuzmina), 49 (garlic/Volodymyr Plysiuk), 49 (roquefort/grafvision), 50 (nails/
Tamara83), 50 (elbow/Steven Frame), 50 (thigh/sozon), 50 (chest/cristovao), 50
(heel/ShotPrime Studio), 50 (palm/Alexandre Zveiger), 51 (two boys/sima), 55
(hacker/Gorodenkoff), 56 (motorbike/Rose Makin), 57 (signing/Kritsana Karakate),
58 (cooking/Rawpixel.com), 58 (referee/Vlad1988), 59 (photographers/Denis
Makarenko), 60 (kitchen staff/wavebreakmedia), 60 (office/Monkey Business
Images), 61 (woman/Stock image), 61 (field/Elenamiv), 62 (vinyl/Rawpixel.com),
65 (dinner/Monkey Business Images), 65 (Mongolian yurt/peachananr), 69 (people
with masks/2p2play), 69 (using tablet/Yakobchuk Viacheslav); Shutterstock
Editorial pp25 (recovery of plane/Depo Photos Via Zuma Wire), 72 (Sidney Poitier/
Anonymous/AP).

Illustrations by: John Haslam pp31, 33; Matthew Hollings p16; Roger Penwill pp11,
36; Willie Ryan p12.

Commissioned photography by: Oxford University Press video stills pp 10 (the
Conversation), 24 (the Conversation), 38 (the Conversation), 52 (Looking at
Language), (the Conversation), 66 (Looking at Language), (the Conversation),

Pronunciation chart artwork by Ellis Nadler